SHEMA

SHEMA

Assemble the Barn Owls

Charla Apana

SHEMA
Assemble the Barn Owls
Copyright © 2020 by Charla Apana
All rights reserved. This book and its use are protected by the copyright laws of the United States of America. This book may not be copied or reprinted for commercial gain or profit. The use of short quotations or the copying of an occasional page for personal or group study is permitted and encouraged. Permission will be granted upon request.
Unless otherwise indicated, all Scripture quotations are taken from the Holy Bible, New International Version®, NIV®. Copyright © 1973, 1978, 1984, 2011 by Biblica, Inc.™ Used by permission of Zondervan. All rights reserved worldwide. www.zondervan.com The "NIV" and "New International Version" are trademarks registered in the United States Patent and Trademark Office by Biblica, Inc.™
Scripture quotations marked (AMP) are taken from the Amplified Bible, Copyright © 1954, 1958, 1962, 1964, 1965, 1987 by The Lockman Foundation. Used by permission. www.Lockman.org.
Scripture quotations marked (KJV) are taken from the King James Version unless otherwise noted. Public Domain.
Scripture quotations marked (MSG) are taken from THE MESSAGE, copyright © 1993, 1994, 1995, 1996, 2000, 2001, 2002 by Eugene H. Peterson. Used by permission of NavPress. All rights reserved. Represented by Tyndale House Publishers, Inc.
Scripture quotations marked (ISV) are taken from the Holy Bible: International Standard Version®. Copyright © 1996–forever by The ISV Foundation. ALL RIGHTS RESERVED INTERNATIONALLY. Used by permission.
Scripture quotations marked (ESV) are taken from the ESV® Bible (The Holy Bible, English Standard Version®), copyright © 2001 by Crossway, a publishing ministry of Good News Publishers. Used by permission. All rights reserved.
Scripture quotations marked (BSB) are taken from the Holy Bible, Berean Study Bible, BSB. Copyright ©2016 by Bible Hub. Used by Permission. All Rights Reserved Worldwide.
Scripture quotations marked (BSB) are taken from the Holy Bible, Berean Study Bible, BSB. Copyright ©2016 by Bible Hub. Used by Permission. All Rights Reserved Worldwide.
Scripture quotations marked (NIrV) are taken from the Holy Bible, New International Reader's Version®, NIrV® Copyright © 1995, 1996, 1998, 2014 by Biblica, Inc.™ Used by permission of Zondervan. All rights reserved worldwide. www.zondervan.comThe "NIrV" and "New International Reader's Version" are trademarks registered in the United States Patent and Trademark Office by Biblica, Inc.™
Scripture quotations marked (GOD'S WORD) are taken from the Holy Bible. GOD'S WORD is a copyrighted work of God's Word to the Nations. Quotations are used by permission. Copyright 1995 by God's Word to the Nations. All rights reserved.

Very truly I tell you, whoever believes in me will do the works I have been doing, and they will do even greater things than these, because I am going to the Father.
—John 14:12 NLT

Contents

PREFACE ix
INTRODUCTION. xi
1   Sh-ma: Are We Listening Yet?. 1
2   *Ruach HaKodesh*: We Need the Breath of God 7
3   Barn Owls: Godly Encounters 17
4   Metamorphosis: Spiritual Transformation Is Painful 29
5   Suicide: Our Trial Becomes Our Ministry. 47
6   Ancestral DNA: Change the Cycle 57
7   Ireland: Reestablish the Covenant Agreement. 71
8   Position of the Heart: Our Battle Has Already Been Won. 95
9   Assemble the Barn Owls: A Call to Shift the Atmosphere of
    Regions. 117
FINAL THOUGHTS 139
ENDNOTES 143

PREFACE

From my heart to yours, I wanted to share our testimony and tell you my story that brought personal revelation to our home, which changed us forever. The prophetic can be extremely rewarding in ways we cannot begin to understand concerning the church and believers.

However, at the same time, it can be very misleading if those involved are not rooted in the word of God and led by the Holy Spirit, and to be tested amongst Men and Women within our faith. One cannot be without the other. I pray you are ready to read this book and understand our Love for the father, his presence, and people.

> *17 'In the last days,' God says, 'I will pour out my Spirit upon all people.*
> *Your sons and daughters will prophesy.*
> *Your young men will see visions,*
> *and your old men will dream dreams.*
> *18 In those days I will pour out my Spirit*
> *even on my servants—men and women alike—*
> *and they will prophesy.*
> —Acts 2:17-18 NLT

INTRODUCTION

HIDE AND SEEK: WHY DOES GOD HIDE THINGS FROM US?

It is God's privilege to conceal things and the king's privilege to discover them.
—Proverbs 25:2 NLT

I WAS TAUGHT AND raised as a Catholic charismatic. When I met my husband, Joseph, at the age of eighteen, we pursued learning more about the evangelical Christian movement. He grew up in a Protestant church on Oahu (Kaumakapili), whereas I grew up in a Catholic church on the island of Kauai. Joseph had a much better understanding of the Holy Spirit than I did. Although I lacked knowledge, I was more sensitive to his prompting. We both decided to unite and grow together in our walk with the Lord.

In my forties, I was challenged to grow deeper in my quest to understand my religious upbringing and where this personal relationship with Jesus stems from. I do not want to start a religious debate about doctrinal differences, so I will stay in my assigned lane because I am in no position to explain theology or go into an in-depth study of it. However, through my personal prayer time, as I asked for wisdom from the Holy Spirit, he led me to the only source that could give me the answers I sought. I followed the trail.

If you are like me, I wanted more. I needed more. I persisted in gaining a better understanding of who adopted me—Jesus—in my faith journey. As Christians, both Joseph and I passionately studied the Bible, which led me to the life of Jesus, his people, and their background. Of course, I traced this back to the Jewish and Hebrew culture. I may not have fully understood all that being a Jew involved, but I wanted to learn more.

Thanks to the resources available to us today on the internet and particularly through Ancestry.com, I found out I have Jewish blood running through my veins. I was shocked. Not only I was blessed to be welcomed as a Gentile, but to be part of this culture was an honor. Nevertheless, most Christians thought of Gentiles as outsiders, invited to be grafted into God's DNA as true believers without Jewish blood. Prior to this, I believed I was not from the Hebrew nation and had no Jewish heritage. But either way, I was welcomed.

"Opening his mouth, Peter said: 'Most certainly I understand now that God is not one to show partiality [to people as though Gentiles were excluded from God's blessing]'" (Acts 10:34 AMP).

Today, this is more than enough as a part of this body of believers because Christ died for all of us. "There is neither Jew nor Gentile, neither slave nor free, nor is there male and female, for you are all one in Christ Jesus. If you belong to Christ, then you are Abraham's seed, and heirs according to the promise" (Galatians 3:28–29).

Prompted by the Holy Spirit, I was led to seek answers about his people and my people and try to ease the tugging of my heart to know more. I learned about the past and present of my race, so I looked into the Hebrew culture, the Jewish community, which left me in tears. I relentlessly pursued what God was hiding from me. It was like a father calling his child to come out and play with him.

Hide and Seek: Why Does God Hide Things from Us?

To think that for my entire life, I was missing out on the Torah, which is the Old Testament written in Hebrew. More importantly, I was missing the way it is understood. I knew of it, but I didn't really put my heart into understanding it. To me, I felt as if I were missing out on the main course of a fine dining experience. Learning the Torah and what it reveals made me feel more complete. This gave me a deeper understanding of the God I fell in love with and how he loves his people, regardless of whether or not I had Jewish blood.

I have asked the Holy Spirit: "How do I explain all of this to others?" I barely understood the Torah and the Hebrew culture myself; I had so much more to learn and discover. I knew enough to explain what the Holy Spirit was revealing to me but felt overwhelmed if I tried to write it all down.

The Holy Spirit responded to me: "Simply share your relationship with me and all that has been transpired between you and Joseph." I was at peace because I could do just that.

At that point, I grew curious about the word *Shema*.

SHEMA

CHAPTER 1

SH-MA: ARE WE LISTENING YET?

Ears that "Shema-hear" and eyes that see—the Lord has made them both.
—Proverbs 20:12

IF THIS BOOK has ended up in your hands, it is because the Holy Spirit is calling you to go deeper and experience a new level in your relationship with him. As we share our story, we hope to encourage you to open up your spiritual eyes and ears to everything that surrounds you. We want you to understand the many ways God is speaking to you on a daily basis in your home and also in your region.

Our revelation from God showed that learning how to listen to the Holy Spirit in numerous ways has been life-changing. I began to research specific Hebrew words: "listening" and "hearing." These two words led me to the Shema, which means hearing and obeying. However, if you truly learn how God loves you first as he extends his presence to you, your listening skills will fall short. This is what God is asking of you.

Love him because he first loved you, and if you do, you will be able to hear him. If you love his people you will be able to hear him; if you love his land, you will be able to hear him.

Listen for God's voice in everything you do, everywhere you go; he's the one who will keep you on track. Don't assume that you know it all. Run to God! Run from evil! Your body will glow with health; your very bones will vibrate with life! Honor God with everything you own; give him the first and the best. Your barns will burst; your wine vats will brim over. But don't, dear friend, resent God's discipline; don't sulk under his loving correction. It's the child he loves that God corrects; a father's delight is behind all this. You're blessed when you meet Lady Wisdom, when you make friends with Madame Insight. She's worth far more than money in the bank; her friendship is better than a big salary. Her value exceeds all the trappings of wealth; nothing you could wish for holds a candle to her. With one hand she gives long life, with the other she confers recognition. (Proverbs 3:6–16)

By listening, you will gain wisdom—not just any wisdom but godly wisdom. My understanding of the Shema is divided into three parts: the Shema, the *Vehayah*, and the *Vaiyomer*.[1] The first part of the Shema begins with a fundamental expression of Jewish belief, this prayer gets its name from here: Shema Yisra'el, which means "hear, Israel." The Shema is an ancient Jewish prayer found in the Torah. This prayer serves as a centerpiece of the morning and evening Jewish prayer services and establishes that there is only one God.

The Shema says that God is personal and requests love from people, Jews, and Gentiles alike, with every facet of their being. It also says that Jews should follow his instructions and allow this love to be witnessed toward others. This Hebrew word "Shema" has two compelling meanings. The first meaning comes from God instructing his people to "listen and obey." The second meaning is from his people asking God or pleading with him to hear us and act on our behalf. "'Shema-hear' my voice when I call, Lord; be merciful and answer me." (Psalms 27:7). "Attention, Israel! God, our God! God the one and only! Love God, your God, with your whole heart: love him with all that's in you, love him with all you've got!" (Deuteronomy 6:4–5 MSG).

The opening verse says, "Listen or pay attention, Oh Israel." Don't let this word enter your ears to be ignored but follow God's commands. In Hebrew, "hearing" and "doing" basically mean the same thing. You must "love the Lord your God" as a response in action.

In the Bible, love is action. If you love someone, it takes action of loyalty and faithfulness. For Israel, love meant faithful obedience, a covenant relationship. Those terms are the laws and commands that will make up the body of the book (Deuteronomy 12–26).

Obedience to these laws was never about legalism or trying to earn God's favor. Obedience in the Old Testament is about "love and listening." An Israelite who loves God can more easily listen to and absorb his teachings and guidance. This is why the words "listen" and "love" are so tightly connected and repeated through these opening speeches of Deuteronomy.

The Shema can keep God's love in your heart and mind. The words of Jesus in the Gospel of John are obviously derived from the Shema: "Whoever has my commands and keeps them is the one who loves me. The one who loves me will be loved by my Father, and I too will love him and show myself to him" (John 14:21). And remember whose love started this whole chain reaction of love leading to obedience. "We love, because he first loved us" (1 John 4:19).

At the end of the day, following Jesus is about love. So we follow him in expressing that love. This word "Shema" resonates with me because it was about "listening and obeying." These two words combined are the Shema and cannot be separated from each other. More importantly, if you are truly listening, you will act on it. Your obedience to trust God in what you hear is the true Shema in practice. This understanding will help you carry out your assignment where God has placed you: in your home and your region. I hope this book will resonate with you and encourage you to observe his promptings in your daily life. So let's move forward and Shema together.

Recognizing the Shema

Growing up as a pastor's kid was very difficult because I had to keep up with certain expectations in our church. There was no room for error in our little town on a small island of Kauai. I felt justified hiding my youthful encounters for the sake of my parents' position in the church and our surrounding communities. However, through my shortcomings, I was convicted because, in the long run, God always had a purpose and plan for my life.

I credit my walk with the Holy Spirit to the opportunity my parents gave me to experience a culture of his presence through worship. My heart savored a rich contentment of peace after every prayer and worship session they hosted. My family's ancestral line of musicians ran through my blood. My dad would play his guitar almost every day before and after he got saved. He was always trying to learn the next worship song so we could sing it together. Thanks to Dad, we developed a family life of ministering to God. My practice in trying to hear God was wrapped in worship. This led me to respond to what he told me to do when I heard him talking to me. I yearned for this lifestyle but didn't quite understand it at a young age.

My relationship with the Holy Spirit started in morning and evening prayer, just like the Shema, but I never realized it. Sometimes at church, when I was not singing, I would constantly talk to Him. Finally, he began to drop thoughts in my mind. This was how we communed.

Even with this relationship, I still had one foot in the world and the other with God. This got me in trouble. Though the Holy Spirit was always gentle and allowed me to fail and learn from every mistake. I accepted that I could not be perfect and realized I needed Jesus. Especially in my failures, I still pursued a life trying to please Him.

Looking back, I wouldn't change any of it, because it made me into the person I am today. My awareness in hearing the Holy Spirit has grown to new levels. God has equipped me to listen, understand, and translate what he is communicating through many situations. As a dreamer, my nights were flooded with dreams. I couldn't even keep up with recording them in the journal that sat next to my bed. I learned early on to ask the Holy Spirit to help me decipher them, and I was relentless in pursuing Him. It was the same for visions, until it eventually became easier to understand them as if a light bulb went off in my head. As soon as the dream or vision was delivered to me, I somehow knew what it was all about.

I also thought about new levels of understanding natural signs and supernatural wonders when God would allow my spirit to receive these. This new level of seeing and hearing him depended on my ability to trust him in this new growth process. He guided me through it all because without the baptism of the Holy Spirit and his gifts, my listening skills could be distorted. I was thankful for this.

When I met Joseph, my husband of more than twenty-eight years, we made it a point to always communicate with one another. We did not learn this overnight, but we have practiced this throughout our married life. Our marriage has been challenging at times, but we worked through it. The hardship we endured caused us to cry out for more of God, bringing us to a place of humility. We began to learn and practice this skill of listening and hearing from God together, which made us want to listen to one another.

This became a fun game that we continually played with the Holy Spirit. As an added plus, we worshiped together, so we could easily enter God's presence through music. We recognized his voice clearly, not as individuals but as a couple. This became very exciting. Over the years as we raised our children, we began to teach them these ways of listening to the Holy Spirit, hoping it would one day resonate with them.

One night, as we studied the Scriptures together, we were crying out to God to show us more of him. Joseph and I were preparing for a Sunday sermon that led us to a life-changing Scripture: "It is God's privilege to conceal things and the king's privilege to discover them." (Proverbs 25:2 NLT). In other words, God allows us to find the hidden things that he himself hides from us. If we want more of his hidden treasures, secrets, and wisdom, we are invited to join him in this discovery. This also helped us recognize that he allows us to reap the benefits of all that we have uncovered and found, not only spiritual but physical treasures as well.

I have heard preachers say that the Father doesn't hide from his children; he hides for them. He hides so that they can seek him out. This has been our premise as we stepped out in faith in this kingdom-minded perspective. As saints, we become modern-day archeologists: willing to uncover or discover whatever God hides. Things of old are revealed to us that are still new because the Father now saves them for our revelation for those who seek them out.

This was a new level of faith for us. Like our encounter with the barn owls that I describe in the upcoming chapters, we just have to find it. Secrets and mysteries are waiting for us.

We pray that you may be able to utilize your gifts from the Holy Spirit to find your personal listening pattern and understand its secrets. You will be amazed at what God has shown us and how widely he communicates if we search it out and are ready to just Shema.

Our journey by faith has become a honeymoon with Him; even in the midst of our storms, God has never left us. You can experience this same reward if you learn to Shema. Listen and obey what he tells you to do and when to do it. You will find a whole new world of the Holy Spirit communicating with you.

Throughout this book, I will switch hats from a storyteller to a teacher, so stay with me as you read and learn about me and my family's journey. You will hear painful struggles; hardships and failures; victories and triumphs; and moments of personal reflections when it comes to a teachable spirit. You will also venture into my world of how God communicates with us and how he can communicate with you.

This book includes interactive lessons to prepare you or your small group to minister over the land and those around them in their everyday lives. We will explore numbers, signs, pictures, symbols, and characteristics about how God spoke to us even through visions and dreams. By sharing our own personal experiences, I hope you can discover your own as well.

This book has been birthed from a pure place of God reigniting a faith walk that needed to be brought back from a dry place. Even though we may walk through the wilderness and perhaps we may feel as if God has left us, he is more present than ever before: He now dwells within us.

CHAPTER 2

RUACH HAKODESH: WE NEED THE BREATH OF GOD

Create in me a pure heart, O God, and renew a steadfast spirit within me. Do not cast me from your presence or take your Holy Spirit from me. Restore to me the joy of your salvation and grant me a willing spirit, to sustain me.
—Psalms 51:10–12

THROUGH READING THE Bible, I witness how God's presence—the Holy Spirit or Ruach HaKodesh—moved among God's people. I began to look and observe my surroundings to see if I could spot him in my everyday life since his presence is invisible. In my research, I found that the Holy Spirit is mentioned ninety times in the Old Testament and demonstrated through his manifest appearance as wind, water, fire, oil, a seal, or other impersonal objects. When Jesus arrived in the New Testament, he became a living manifestation of the Holy Spirit here on Earth.

I want you to do the following right now to get a practical sense or feeling of his presence. I can talk to you all about him, but this will help you understand him tangibly. Pray before you start this and ask the Ruach HaKodesh to come and help you feel and hear him. Go to a quiet spot, like your bathroom, and shut the door. Take out the recorder on your phone and record your deep breathing. When you are ready to begin, inhale deeply through your nose and open your mouth as you exhale. Make sure you record this "ha" sound in the lowest possible tone, extending that sound as long as you can. Do that three times. After recording and before you listen to it, say these words: "Let your presence, God, breathe through me." After you do this, sit in silence for a while, just listening to it. It will impact you in a tangible way. That's how I can describe the Ruach HaKodesh, the Holy Spirit. God's presence is in his breath, and his breath is in your soul, so with his presence, you grow in these listening skills throughout your life.

At fifteen years old, I would lay on my back under a small shaded tree outside my bedroom window. I stared up into the beautiful blue Hawaiian sky, trying to talk to the Lord. I said, "Where are you? Just tell me how to spend quality time alone with you. If I can't hear you, how can you talk to me?"

I was introduced to the Ruach HaKodesh before my teens. I would go with my parents to a prayer meeting and be a backup singer for my dad as he played guitar. I watched this charismatic group passionately worship and enthusiastically pray for our island and for one another. During the gospel part, I ran to the food table and ate while listening to impactful testimonies as the Ruach HaKodesh powerfully engaged with them. I really did not understand what was happening, but the emotions overwhelmed me. It took me some time to learn to hear and feel him on my own and to see him physically manifest in others. I had to discern if it was Him. I began hearing his voice echoing in my thoughts as my own voice, so it was hard for me to distinguish at times. At some point, I realized I needed better discernment because not only did I hear the Ruach HaKodesh in the sound of my voice, but the enemy's voice and my very own personal thoughts sounded like my voice as well.

I realized God's presence was an invisible energy, a soft or a powerful wind. My mind usually would not understand it, but my heart and body could feel it. This was my faith in action.

I waited to meet with him as my normal expectancy. I wanted to see when and where I would experience him in different ways other than in a worship service at church with other Christians. I wanted to see if I could catch him in a way that was not invisible but manifested in nature, sounds, animals, and unbelievers. I believed that his presence hid just so that I would seek him out and be amazed.

It took practice to be in sync with the Ruach HaKodesh and to understand how he would maneuver within my situations. One of the keys to identifying how he works in situations through people's lives was spending time with him, which was an incredible experience to witness.

While searching for a deeper understanding of the Ruach HaKodesh, I was led to research the original Hebrew script, sometimes called "Paleo Hebrew." I then found myself directed to the Torah. In Judaism, this is considered the divine revelation to the Jewish people: which is God's revealed teaching or guidance for humankind.

Like me, you may be questioning where our Christian roots came from. A good place to start is with Jesus. I began to follow his genealogy, and many questions were answered. I was led through time, trying to understand that there was more than Western Christian culture. I wanted to know more about Messianic Jews or the Judeo Christians and the original language of Jesus.

I began to look at the etymological dictionary of the Hebrew language. This language was written in Paleo Hebrew in the form of pictograms. These give a much greater understanding in picture form because you must study in depth to decode the interpretation.

I found out that Hebrew text is considered an action-based language, which was never meant to be read just for a person's thought process but to be used to provoke encouragement to participate and be involved. My search kept on focusing on the Holy Spirit, so I pressed forward as he was leading me. I focused on how the ancient text explained Ruach HaKodesh to us. I needed to search it from the point of view of God's perspective in allowing us to have this advantage and why.

I started by looking at the word Ruach HaKodesh, which as I said, means the Holy Spirit. The words "Holy Spirit" were not found in the Torah; the concept arrived when the New Testament was formatted and translated by the Greeks.

Stay with me as I explain all this to you and try not to get lost down the rabbit hole of information. What I am saying will help you understand the originality of God's invitation, an invitation to become closer to him before Christ was manifested in human form to us. I was in tears as I learned and understood his secrets. This brought about a confidence in knowing how detailed God is as he wants us to learn how much he loved us before the world was created.

The Torah is a Hebrew word meaning "to instruct."[2] The Torah refers to the five books of Moses in the Hebrew Old Testament (Genesis, Exodus, Leviticus, Numbers, and Deuteronomy). The Torah and Bible are sacred. Although it only constitutes the first five books of the Bible, you can learn so much when you explore it.

The Holy Spirit described in the Torah is Ruach Elohim or the Spirit of God. Again, Ruach HaKodesh and Ruach Elohim are the Spirit of God. The pictogram you see here is the original word picture for Ruach HaKodesh:[3] WΔየ⅃ ᗺየ٩

These symbolic writings are read from right to left. The first symbol is the head of a person, the second symbol is a nail, and the third resembles a ladder, which is a fence. These three pictures have specific meanings. The head means the leader, master, or the prince. The nail means an iron nail to fasten or secure. The fence means to separate, protect, or to cut off and be a sanctuary.

The second part is HaKodesh which is described in four pictograms and which again reads from right to left.[4] WΔየ⅃ The first picture looks like a three-prong comb, but it is described as a stickman with his arms raised in worship. The second picture shows the back of a head, which would be a person faced with a decision to enter through that open doorway, which is the next picture, or a triangle. The fourth picture is of a capital W. The bottom of the W has two points while the top has three points. These three points symbolize that a person can stand on either side but cannot stand in the middle. In other words, they will have to choose which side or road they will travel down. The road to the right will bring you to eternal life with God. The road to the left is a road to selfishness and pleasure, which brings a separation from God and a life of damnation.

To sum up the meaning of the pictogram, you, as the leader of your home, the person in charge, need to get serious to secure your stance in God and to hold tight as you follow him. You will have to separate your worldly desires to protect your heart so you can stay in a place of peace with him. When you worship him, you will always have the opportunity to choose life or death, he will never force you. If you chose life, he will invite you into a special room where his Ruach HaKodesh will reveal his full identity to you. Here, you will gain the wisdom, the understanding, and the knowledge of God fully so that you can walk out your life successfully, not only for yourself but for others. As you enter in this place, you will be able to sit with the Ruach Hakodesh, who will place a stamp of approval on you, a seal of great worth. It's a seal of understanding your spiritual authority, not only on Earth but in the heavenly places and in the unseen.

Incredibly, this pictogram revealed all of that.[5] Once I understood this, I honored the process of his invitation through this doorway of secrets. These symbols gave a deep understanding of the sacredness of ancient times that God has given his people access to allow his presence, his Ruach Hakodesh, to enter into our lives if we choose him. When Jesus was born, his blood became the active manifestation on Earth, the Ruach HaKodesh that transforms lives. When he ascended into heaven, he left us Ruach HaKodesh to aid us in our faith journey. Ruach means "breath or wind." HaKodesh means to "behold and pay attention to God's presence, which is the Holy Spirit the revealer."[6]

Within the Arabic documents and many Messianic writings, Ruach HaKodesh indicates the phrase to be translated as "the Holy Spirit." Ruach is another way of describing God's presence. his presence is everywhere if we observe and notice him. Normally, he is invisibly near but not observed because we are too busy or distracted. Think of this: When we normally bring forth our voice, his breath actually comes forth from inside us. We become his express voice if we allow him to move within us. God's breath and his spoken words convey his presence. This is why we need to choose the road that brings life and not death.

If you can hear someone breathing or talking to you, they are present. We all have experienced someone's character or spirit that fills the room and draws everyone's attention. This is the power of God in our voice. If we are not careful, we can abuse our power and authority so that God removes us from his presence. Sometimes we are distracted and caught up in our everyday business. King David knew about God's presence and feared that it would depart from him because of the wrong choices he made that displeased God. But he prayed, "Do not take Your Ruach HaKodesh from me." (See Psalm 51:11.)

The understanding of the Shema can be activated here. Many times, I am easily distracted by my own desires and wants from within my prayer and seal my ears to hearing his voice because I want what I want. Ruach HaKodesh wants to be involved and lead us in our lives, especially in our prayers, but we can become so consumed with our words of passion that we may miss the mark of God's prayer, which is exactly how the enemy can distract us. We need to come to God in a place of Shema so we can agree with him.

Could we have become like the babbling tower in Genesis 11 where the people just wanted to make a name for themselves?

The Tower of Babylon

"There was a time when the entire earth spoke a common language with an identical vocabulary. As people migrated westward, they came across a plain in the region of Shinar and settled there. They told each other, 'Come on! Let's burn bricks thoroughly.' They used bricks for stone and tar for mortar. Then they said, 'Come on! Let's build ourselves a city and a tower, with its summit in the heavens, and let's make a name for ourselves so we won't be scattered over the surface of the whole earth'" (Genesis 11:1–4 ISV).

We need to reflect and slow down when we pray. We can easily become spiritual whiners, complainers, and worry warts and present selfish ambition, all in the name of God, because we think that will make our prayers work. We can even use Scripture to back up our motives. God's thoughts are higher than ours, so we need to listen to him.

Sometimes our prayer should be as simple as repeating the Lord's Prayer, just as Jesus showed us. Could we just be babbling? Where has the honeymoon with Jesus gone? When you are in love with someone, you listen. Take the time to Shema in our worship and our prayer, and let's stop the babbling when we don't have time to just sit in his presence, to wait and listen.

We all have the ability to see objects as larger than they are. In the spiritual realm, God will magnify words, numbers, objects, or whatever he sees fit to get your attention. Once you reach this place of listening to God, objects around you will be magnified. Pay attention to everything because the Ruach HaKodesh is always talking to us, using whatever is around us. You just have to practice seeing what is magnified to you. In your spiritual journey, you need to exercise your spiritual senses and constantly teach yourself how to read how God speaks in numerous ways.

The Ruach HaKodesh plays with us and communicates in different ways, like a puzzle that needs to be put together by you. First, we need to see those magnified pieces that God illuminates around us all the time. When we recognize our surroundings more carefully, this aids us in our faith journey. These clues are strategic and intentional tools to help us pray what he wants us to pray and lead us into spontaneous prophetic worship with fresh proclamations over our regions.

One of our first magnifying processes began in our home with our children. When our kids would come home from outings, sometimes they acted differently with a very harsh attitude. I questioned if this was my kid or a spirit. Their emotions were not their own. Right away, we recognized the issue and kept a watchful eye on them. As an intercessor, sometimes I could be incredibly detailed in my prayers. It became religious at times, but along the way, I realized that it was my own agenda and not God's.

Numbers, elements, catch phrases, movies, animals, conversations, music, and even incidents can all be a broader view of how God speaks if you are paying attention. We cannot keep God locked up in a box. God will use all your skills to help you navigate and learn how to understand what he magnifies to you so you can understand the translation and ultimate meaning. He did this to me with my career.

While studying at the University of Hawaii, I was unsure what area of teaching I should pursue. As time went on, I discovered I had a heart for high maintenance students who were emotionally unstable with learning disabilities, to name a few. This passion led me to become a certified enrichment teacher.

These students were traumatized and lost in the school system. Home life was hard, and school was confusing. They struggled to cope. Many of my students were in a mental crisis and could not communicate because they themselves didn't know what was happening. Socially, they were not at peace, and learning was the last thing on their minds. They had a hard time transitioning, which never went well. I was at a standstill. I cried out to God to help me understand because I could not share God with them, as this was a public school. Since I was not allowed to talk about Jesus, I began to model him as best as I could without words.

I needed the Ruach HaKodesh to help me communicate with them. I needed to find the right timing or window of opportunity to help them to trust me, even if I did not share my faith. I knew God had me in this position for a reason. I began to train myself to look for signs in their behaviors, their friendships, their academics, and especially their art drawings. I also watched how they communicated with their parents, other adults, teachers, and students and began a Ruach HaKodesh assessment. I did this daily.

In 2013, when the opportunity came along, I was offered a position as a childcare director at the Boys and Girls Club. This job gave me insights into thousands of students across our county, and to be honest, I had to take my gifts from Ruach HaKodesh to new levels, especially since we weren't allowed to speak of our religion. Modeling Jesus became a skilled process I learned while keeping a professional title and respecting their own religious preferences.

Not only did I practice this listening skill at work, but I began to make it a lifestyle. I became a keen observer socially and spiritually. So back to my point. My children would come home from school with an entitled attitude. I would question where their attitude came from. Ruach HaKodesh prompted me to ask questions, such as who they were hanging out with. I began to pray for those kids who influenced my kids. I took authority over those situations because I had identified them. We watched local and world news nightly to see where God would have us pray. We knew that the reports showed a clear indication of what was happening in the spiritual realm over our city. We didn't get into a warring spirit of prayer but focused on speaking life into the atmosphere.

I know we hate watching the negative news, but we can learn so much about what we are facing on today's front lines regarding the supernatural forces that are trying to battle us. Pay close attention to situations within your state, city, and your neighborhood. This understanding will show you what your city is facing, giving you an understanding of the overall atmosphere.

We always inquired of the Ruach HaKodesh for understanding. We began to see a routine that he used with us. He made certain words known to us in our spirits that were magnified when they were presented to us.

For example, when reading Scripture, a specific word or phrase would stand out to me or to Joseph. Later in the day, a person on the radio would be talking about it. My daughter would come home and mention the same word. This type of listening became clearer each time as we paid attention to everything around us.

Ruach HaKodesh will teach you and prompt you to see these clues when he knows you are looking for them. And when you are looking for them, you will experience godly encounters. While reading, pay attention to the italicized words in the Scriptures that I share. The Lord sometimes speaks to us in italics. You will find this throughout the pages of this book, but he will show you in your own way. Have an expectant spirit, and he will show you things that will amaze you. Let God's Ruach HaKodesh into your life and watch what happens.

CHAPTER 3

BARN OWLS: GODLY ENCOUNTERS

All around us we observe a pregnant creation. The difficult times of pain throughout the world are simply birth pangs. But it's not only around us; it's within us. The Spirit of God is arousing us within. We're also feeling the birth pangs. These sterile and barren bodies of ours are yearning for full deliverance. That is why waiting does not diminish us,
any more than waiting diminishes a pregnant mother. We are enlarged in the waiting. We, of course, don't see what is enlarging us. But the longer we wait,
the larger we become, and the more joyful our expectancy.
—Romans 8:22–25 MSG

ROMANS 8:22 REVEALED so much to me when we encountered a supernatural manifestation with a barn owl outside my window late one night after a visit from Ray Hughes. God used Ray Hughes to reignite our calling, and we understood this Scripture better after his visit. That passage has been in our mental vat for more than eight years. Each time we read it, we understand more and more of its power. Joseph and I have intense conversations on these verses and on how they are broken down to bring fresh revelation. This Scripture explains so much about God's call. God has established each individual to be pregnant with a specific destiny and a vibration, a sound that needs to be birth. You have a unique sound that cannot be copied. It is like a puzzle piece that cannot be duplicated.

God waits and hopes that we will realize that we carry power to bring forth life to the dead things on Earth but also to the dead things in a person's life. We are the carriers of new life. Your sound can bring an atmospheric change. Pregnancy is not easy, and the birthing process can be long and hard.

In order to become pregnant, we must first be in a relationship. The relationship leads to love, which leads to intimacy. And intimacy it can bring about new life.

The Earth and its people are in different stages of pregnancy, and those who have experienced birth need to heed the call, the call to be spiritual midwives to those who may be spiritually pregnant. This is a call to help comfort and soothe the atmosphere with God's peace to bring forth a spiritual child, a spiritual child of ministry for God's people. Ray Hughes acted as a spiritual midwife that directed and encouraged us to push through the birthing process. This became a revelation to us abroad. As a mother of six children, I can attest to the birthing process. It feels so good to deliver your child after nine months in the womb.

We are a pregnant civilization waiting to bring forth something new. Where have the spiritual midwives gone? Where are the pregnant carriers of God's new life? People are hurting, lost, and aimlessly following the next fad and trend. We have become a loud, opinionated world, where everyone has to tell their side and everyone needs to be heard.

People are fighting just to be right, fighting and debating just to be heard, and if you don't agree with them, you become an enemy. People are lawless and justifying everything they do by a twisted doctrine of self. This is a selfish pride that contradicts the positive wholesomeness of communities and, of course, the living Word of God. We are now living in a world that if you don't conform to the ways of the world, you are an enemy. It is very twisted, but God's hope is arising in those who will listen and obey, who will Shema. A calling is happening, and the bridegroom Jesus is crying out for his bride. The calling is for midwives of the faith who will encourage and direct those who are willing to be pregnant with and for the gospel of Jesus Christ.

We first met Ray Hughes back in Las Vegas more than a decade ago on November 16, 2008. If you are a worship leader, you may have come across Ray's daughter Ramey and Brain Whalen who wrote and sang that iconic song "Praises Rise" at The Call Nashville in 2007. My girls loved that song so much they made her a green bracelet to wear whenever she sang. On occasion, Joseph played the bass for them every time Ramey and Bryan were in town to lead worship at our church. It was a beautiful time of growth. This family made such an impact on my home. Ray's biblical insights, wisdom, and storytelling, combined with his knowledge of revival history and music, holds a special place in our hearts.

Ray would host conferences as the main guest speaker. Joseph and I never forgot what he impressed on our hearts, which resonated with us till this day. He demonstrated how the vibration of sound has such great impact that it will react and respond.

He shared from his book *Sound of Heaven, Symphony of Earth* about a sound coming from heaven that will invade the Earth. If you have an ear to hear it, you will be able to respond and come into agreement to release a harmony that will change the atmosphere, a symphony of God's beauty. When that sound from heaven combines with your sound and the Earth, it will resonate to become an instrument within the Earth. You will resound with a glorious song coming from inside the Earth because you are part of the Earth. This was a huge revelation of an atmosphere shift that was waiting to take place in our lives.

These were authentic sounds of our own personal worship. Your vibration of sound can travel far, causing a wavelength of worship that can affect the land. Call it God's crafted work of art, making us a unique distribution of sound. No one has the same sound; no one has the same fingerprint. This personal expression can be combined with other sounds from other people to bring an incredible revelation for us to hear within our soul. We really didn't understand what that meant at the time, but later we totally understood it.

That night at the conference, Ray did something on the platform that blew our minds. He picked up a guitar and started to tune it and placed it back down on its stand. He then told the soundman to turn up the sound of the guitar in the house and instructed him to make his voice loud in the monitor.

He then began to sing, and as his voice echoed throughout the sanctuary, the guitar on the stand reacted or responded to his voice by vibrations. Ray's voice echoed throughout the sanctuary. His soundwaves bounced off the guitar, which vibrated in the key of his voice. It was harmony. The guitar reacted to the sound of his voice as if someone strummed it. Ray even sang a different key, and the guitar followed his vibration. He called it God's song and said that Gods vibration sustains the whole Earth. Ray mentions when your song, your vibration, can come in agreement with God, we can create a sustainable sound to heal and to respond to his love in ways we don't understand.

Ray Hughes deposited something in our spirits that night ten years ago. It took a full decade of growth for Joseph and I to understand what we needed to do personally. Ray had a huge impact on what would transpire in our future, which you will read about in the coming chapters.

Ray Hughes

Much later, we reconnected with Papa Ray in an incredible way. I was up late one night, questioning the Lord, asking, *Is this what my life has amounted to?* I was now in my forties in a huge four-bedroom house with my six kids, and life felt somewhat complete. *There must be more,* I thought. My relationship with Joseph was beyond blessed, finances were balanced, and home life was great. We were all together, safe and healthy, although we had our struggles. Still, I wondered, *Have I lost track of my divine purpose?*

Thoughts swirled in my mind. *What had become of me, my husband, and our talented, anointed musical family?* We were hiding our gifts and talents under a bushel, settling for a mundane life. I also felt that this routine life kept my family safe from any spiritual attacks from the enemy. We were a family of worshippers, and our comfort grew on us. If this was

God's will, I was fine with it, but my heart and my soul were crying out for a confirmation.

Unbeknownst to me, this was all about to change. God was not going to answer me by an audible voice but by a physical manifestation through nature that I was not expecting.

We went through so many obstacles and felt our family was dysfunctional. I am sure many families believe the same thing, but I wondered who could be as messed up as we were. I felt that we had so many issues that we dealt with almost daily. I wondered if God could ever get us back on track so that we were walking out the destiny he had for us. Each one of my children had their own set of challenges, which I had to help them learn to navigate. That has been a learning curve to this day. God reminded me I just needed to be the best Mom I could be for them and love them through it. But I needed some kind of response. Where was God?

I waited for some audible voice from the Lord that never came, and he opted for a Facebook notification from my iPhone that chimed in. The notification was from some ad concerning the stars and the mysterious sounds from outer space. I thought, *Okay, Lord, what do you have to say to me through Facebook about the stars?*

Curious, I opened the notification and the audio recording, which were sounds from NASA recorded from outer space. This caught my attention. When listening to them, I was in awe of the grandeur of my Creator. The fear of the Lord overcame me. I instantly knew my place in God's kingdom and understood how small I was but how big he makes me. I was in total fear but in total contentment, knowing I was part of his master plan of creation.

The video spoke about sounds that can travel through space but cannot technically be heard by the normal human ear. These sounds exist in the form of electromagnetic vibrations that travel through space in different wave lengths. Eager to know more about why God was leading me here, I continued to read. NASA created a special spacecraft to detect these sounds from outer space and converted them for our human ears to hear. This grabbed my attention, and I knew God was leading me to go deeper in understanding it all.

The entire time while I was reading and listening to these sounds, only one person strongly came to mind: Ray Hughes. I was so moved by these sounds, I decided to share them with him, so I tagged his name from my Facebook account. To my surprise, he responded quickly. I was not expecting him to respond so quickly if at all.

He messaged me, saying my timing was perfect because at that moment, he was star gazing in the middle of the night. I got goosebumps and began to cry because we both experienced a God moment. Two different time zones and two different countries and God's presence was in the center of it. Surprisingly, he was in the Emerald Isle, the land of Ireland. But Ray did not know that I had been praying and feeling drawn to Ireland for years. I knew God was up to something, that he was preparing us for something amazing.

I would dream of Ireland and envision myself there. I would weep for its people and feel a tugging of my heart to just get there. I didn't know when or how, but Joseph and I knew we needed to get there, and God was going to do it.

We watched movies and documentaries of Ireland. Advertisements and round-trip offers popped up on TV. I told Joseph that God was preparing to deposit some kind of spiritual anointing in us or that we would deposit something in the land. As time went on, we decided to just call it out that we were going by faith. This would be the honeymoon we really never had. So we began to dream and thank the Lord that he would get us there. It was no coincidence that Ray was in Ireland when we connected on Facebook. God was at work.

A couple of weeks later, Ray told us he was coming to Seattle and wanted to meet up. I mentioned it to Joe, and we both agreed that we would travel to see him no matter where in Seattle he would be. I texted Ray, and he told us where to meet him—at a church just three miles from our home. The Lord was definitely orchestrating our connection, and we just needed to do our part and follow through.

We had a great time reconnecting at this worship conference. Ray told us that he and his wife Denise had been hosting tours to the Celtic lands of Ireland for a while. They felt drawn to this area since the '90s. Interestingly,

Ireland's past has a great impact and influence on the world through their music, literature, and their export of world leaders and culture shapers. He told us that they hosted tours to share stories of powerful revivals and revivalists in Christian history, and they called their trip the Heart of David tour. We had no idea Ray and Denise were doing this! We haven't been in contact with them or even followed them since 2008, and it was 2018!

We began to tell him how Ireland was on our hearts and expressed our love for the land and its people. He asked us if we were joining him on his tour. But since the tour was previously planned, unfortunately it filled up fast. We told him that we felt strongly about going even if we couldn't get on his tour. He agreed.

Ray responded, "It looks like God wants just the both of you and no one else on this trip. If so, then you just should go with it." We were going to get there one way or another. He then gave us some vital advice. "Pay close attention to the elements when you get there."

That night, at the conference, Ray took the stage and preached a little and told encouraging stories. He sang a couple of songs to the congregation that I recorded on my iPhone. We left feeling so full of God's love, as if we were reaching a new level of communicating and listening to God.

Supernatural Encounters
2018

When Joseph and I got home after the conference, I was thinking about the entire night. I was thanking God how wonderful it was that he never forgot us.

Just past midnight, I changed into my pajamas and stretched out on my bed to relax, reflecting our nights events. I took out my phone and replayed a song Ray sang while playing guitar. Outside an animal screeched.

That screech scared me. I stopped the song of Ray playing on my iPhone to listen more closely since it was in the middle of the night. My bedroom window was open with the blinds drawn, so I waited but heard nothing. So I continued to listen to Ray's song. Sure enough, the screech echoed from outside again.

I paused Ray's song, and again, it was silent. I waited awhile to see if I could hear more clearly. It sounded like some kind of night creature in the woods. I thought quickly, *Why do I only hear that screeching sound when I play Ray's song?* In a millisecond, I realized this screeching was responding to Ray's voice and the vibrations of his guitar. I totally ignored that thought and tried rationalizing it away. As a test, I turned Ray's song off again, and the screeching stopped. I don't know why I was so skeptical. I had heard far more mysterious stories of great signs and wonders of God's encounters that happened in people's lives over the years. This was no different; it was just happening to me.

So for ten minutes, I sat in silence, and no sound came from the woods. I began to play Ray's song, and there it was again: a screeching echo that grew closer to my bedroom window. It wasn't like any normal sound I have ever heard; it was a deep screeching and it scared me, to be honest.

Curious, I did a quick internet search to see if I could find out what kind of animal it was. It was a barn owl. These beautiful white owls are in the animated movie *The Guardians*.

I replayed the screeching that I found on the internet from my iPhone, and the owl outside responded. However, the owl outside screeched even more intensely.

The more I played the sound, the closer and louder the owl came until it was right outside my bedroom window. I ran downstairs and opened my sliding door to see if I could spot him on our neighbors' roof as no tall trees were near my bedroom window. But I saw nothing and ran back upstairs. I said, *God, is this you?* I suddenly felt his presence like a fire over my room and his Holy Spirit flooded my heart.

Tears ran down my face. I thought, *Wow, God, you are using an owl to get my attention as it responds to Ray Hughes's song.* Still in awe, I searched for the characteristics of a barn owl in the Pacific Northwest at night and why they make these screeches like a dying animal crying for help.

I found that the male is in a deep longing and searches for his mate. As I was reading, I was so engulfed in the Rauch HaKodesh that each word was a divine revelation. He needed me to understand, not only with my mind but with my heart and soul. I cried the entire time as I understood spiritually that God was calling me and longing for me to hear and respond.

The owl makes this screeching as if it is in deep pain. His cry for a mate comes from the deepest part of its inner soul. He wants a mate that can respond with the same intensity of love form her to him. He looks for a bride to join in his call in his mission to become one. When they find each other, they can start multiplying. This metaphor was speaking to me as if a birthing were about to take place in our lives. God was trying to get my attention. The owl screeches and calls until the call is returned by another who waits and responds, allowing them to unite.

I continued to read on the mating process. These owls usually start in late winter and early spring, but it was now August. This did not seem peculiar because of the abnormal seasons in the last decade. I immediately knew in my bones it was a God encounter, a Ruach HaKodesh moment, a Shema moment.

In a millisecond, God was calling me to draw closer to him, closer than I could ever imagine. He was looking for me, his bride. God was screeching for me to come to him, just like the owl that searches for his bride.

This owl was moving outside its normal season of mating and away from the familiar patterns it exhibited for generations. What was previously out of order was shifting into the new. The owls were adapting to the new. The land was shifting, and the atmosphere was changing, and the owl went along with it. Just like the owl, we needed to shift and flow with it as well and follow what God had in store for us in this season.

This spoke loudly to us as we needed to prepare to adapt to the changing seasons of what God was doing by drawing closer to the Rauch HaKodesh. We needed to pay attention and work on our listening skills, Shema, and to what was around us. Start this skill of listening, watching, and learning. Pay attention to how the land around us shifts and talks to us in its own ways in the weather patterns because the Earth and nature are speaking to us.

God is trying to get our attention with the animals of the land as they are in sync with one another. We can see this through the transitions of the seasons and climate change. The Rauch HaKodesh was confirming this.

Ray's visit with us was catapulting us into the new things of God and connecting us with the elements to aid us in our spiritual authority from God.

We were coming to a different level of understanding and listening that had to do with our worship, with the Earth, and with our listening skills and how we would continue to ask for his wisdom through it all. God was recruiting us as spiritual barn owls in our region. We realized there were more spiritual barn owls out there, so we prayed that the Lord would connect us with them. God was showing us how connected we are to nature.

After meeting with Ray and this encounter with the barn owl, the Lord began to download prior events that we experienced with the Rauch HaKodesh and nature related to worship and how God responds to us. One day, Joseph and I were casually sitting in the backyard with his guitar worshiping and praying together. We were surrounded by tall pine trees, and the atmosphere was still, no wind at all. You could hear a pin drop.

Then slowly a gentle wind brushed up against us. We both knew it was the Rauch HaKodesh. Joseph continued to play his guitar, and the trees began to sway slowly in his timing while we sang. We continued to worship and fell in sync with what God was doing in that moment. We worshiped with the wind and sat in complete silence as Joe stopped playing. Amazingly, when he stopped playing, the wind stopped as well. We realized the power that God had placed in us if we sync ourselves with God's plan. We both teared up. God did something in our neighborhood that day. We took up residency in our region and took responsibility for the land. This was available to all believers. We stood in faith for better things for the neighborhood.

We called things into existence in our region by agreeing with God for new life. Hebrews 11:1 calls forth this hope: "Now faith brings our hopes into reality and becomes the foundation needed to acquire the things we long for. It is all the evidence required to prove what is still unseen" (TPT).

The Lord immediately brought this revelation to our minds and told us to respect the land and its surroundings and come into agreement with it.

In 1996, when I was twenty-one, my parents took us on a five-city tour through Texas. We traveled to many churches and hospitals, holding worship services and ministering to people. It was a great time of learning and working with the Rauch HaKodesh. But there was one place we went made a huge impact on our faith while on this tour. It was an outdoor concert near a huge riverfront property, and God showed us he was there. The river was running and the trees rustled around us. It was quite beautiful.

My dad led the entire choir in worship. While we were singing a song from Ron Kenoly, "Let Everything that Has Breath Praise the Lord," the wind grew stronger and stronger. It scared us at first, but everyone paid attention. The louder we sang, the stronger the wind blew. Nature was responding to and agreeing with us. I didn't understand it then, but today I do. We were in sync with God and nature. I thought maybe we would be swooped up into heaven. That day, we felt a touch from God. We came into agreement with whatever God was doing on that land, that soil, and in that region. It took that specific sound from us, from Hawaii, to align with God to birth a manifestation of new life in that region.

From that moment on, we had a tangible experience of connecting with the Earth without even realizing what was happening at the time. Psalm 105:6 came alive: "Let everything that has breath praise the Lord."

The trees were praising the Lord too. Why? Because they also have breath. Everything that God made that is living will praise the Lord. This opened a new level of understanding to us. We were changing atmospheres long before we knew what that even meant because we trusted in God who brought forth an anointing that had been collecting within us over the years.

Once we had this revelation, we understood why God was sending us to Ireland. We believed we were God's spiritual barn owls to sing and play worship over the land, to be used by God to sound an alarm to those who have an ear and a heart to listen, a call to wake up the dry bones on the land. We were gearing up to reestablish a covenant agreement concerning our faith with those who traveled the path before us.

While planning our trip, everything fell into place. We prayed and pulled all our songs together and trusted that the Lord would lead us to specific places. We weren't invited to any churches, and we didn't have any speaking engagements. We just had a plan to drive north and do what God told us to do. The plan was to go to each site that God led us to and prophetically worship and sing over the land. We also waited to see how the elements would respond to us, which they did. There was no honorarium, no group of worshipers to join in, no concert hall, no audience, just us and the Rauch HaKodesh and his agenda. Just the two barn owls, letting our vibrations echo throughout the land. Why play instruments and sing over the land? Because the land is part of us. We were created from the dust. We are to unite with all the natural things. Man is the first root created; we manifest the image and authority of God. We see in the Bible we are one with the Earth. "At the time God made Earth and Heaven, before any grasses or shrubs had sprouted from the ground—God hadn't yet sent rain on Earth, nor was there anyone around to work the ground (the whole Earth was watered by underground springs)—God formed Man out of dirt from the ground and *blew into his nostrils the breath of life.* The Man came alive—a living soul!" (Genesis 2:5–7 MSG, emphasis added)

I think we are the modern day Davids. The Bible tells us of a shepherd boy who knew the importance of worshiping God in the fields before being crowned king. As he played his instrument and sang over the fields, he was offering his unique prophetic sound, his vibrations to change and prepare a place of spiritual birth of victory.

David prepared the land as he ministered in worship to God over the fields. What came next was the slaying of Goliath the giant. David sang on that land for years before he came into contact with Goliath. The shepherd knew the importance of shifting atmospheres. How fascinating to think we are to be used to tear down the Goliaths of our regions by understanding this.

CHAPTER 4

METAMORPHOSIS: SPIRITUAL TRANSFORMATION IS PAINFUL

*Therefore, if anyone is in Christ, he is a new creation.
The old has passed away; behold, the new has come.*
—2 Corinthians 5:17 ESV

IT IS NOT easy to Shema all that God has for us, which is why personal transformation must take place. Not only did I need a metamorphosis but my entire family did as well. My transformation took me from an immature state of mind to a wiser, mature woman of faith. The stages of transformation will never stop; it is an ongoing process. It's like a caterpillar that transforms into a cocoon and then emerges as a beautiful butterfly, or the tadpole that changes into a frog.

Creation offers us examples of manifestations of rebirth into something entirely new. The caterpillar cannot stop its transition into a butterfly. The tadpole cannot halt its progression into a frog. The duckling cannot stifle its transformation into its mature appearance as an elegant swan. These creatures were made to grow, change, and adapt. Each stage is a shedding of the old to help you into the new. True followers will experience this; like the butterfly, the frog, and the swan, this is a process that God wants us to grow through.

Our instinct is to resist change. Many times, if it doesn't make sense to us, we wonder how it can be good for us, especially if it's uncomfortable or painful. In these seasons of learning, we felt afraid and lonely. This attitude, however, can slow God's process. Many Christians want to avoid growing pains and the resulting transformation. Following God is the best decision you can ever make, but it's not always a bed of roses. Trusting him through your personal metamorphosis brings you greater understanding. The trials will come, but at least, he will be beside you through it all.

The Rauch HaKodesh helped us walk through all the hardship that we experienced, and believe it or not, many times it was not fair. But when we embraced these painful trials and unexpected hurts, God released a specific anointing of authority on us to be curse breakers. We became curse breakers over those circumstances that tried to destroy our family through generations. This also gave us spiritual keys from God to understand and use the wisdom gained from those trials to help others.

However, we did not expect the hurt, the pain, and the trials that would come from our fellow Christians. It destroyed us! In fact, it killed our spirits. We had no idea how to handle what was to come. Who would have thought our metamorphosis was by the people who we trusted the most.

We found comfort and wisdom in Matthew 23:11–12: "Do you want to stand out? Then step down. Be a servant. If you puff yourself up, you'll get the wind knocked out of you. But if you're content to simply be yourself, your life will count for plenty" (MSG).

I guess this is when we got the wind knocked out of us.

My Dream

"Deep calls to deep in the roar of your waterfalls; all your waves and breakers have swept over me" (Psalm 42:7). I had this recurring dream and would wake up in a sweat, sometimes in a panic, gasping for air. It seemed

Metamorphosis: Spiritual Transformation Is Painful

as if I could never reach the end of this dream because I would die before the entire dream was revealed to me. It felt so real that I could die in my sleep if I didn't wake.

I dreamed I was on a beautiful colonial ship and could see a tremendous waterspout tornado in the distance. Strong gusty winds blew hard, pushing this waterspout toward me. It gained momentum, sucking the ship into the eye of this storm.

Aggressive waves tossed the ship back and forth like a leaf in the water. Above me, lightning streaked across the dark gray sky as thunder echoed loudly behind me. Soaked, shaking, and freezing I began to panic, while the waves grew larger and larger. I could hear God saying to me, "Hold on, there is no way around this storm. You need to face it head on!"

I tried to secure myself with a piece of rope that dangled down in front of me from an already torn sail. I secured my feet under another piece of rope nailed to the floorboard of the ship. Many more massive waterspout tornados were closing in all around me. In the distance, my boat was gravitating toward a black hole that opened up on top of the ocean, trying to swallow me.

The last thing I heard was a deep vibration as the ship lifted and capsized, spiraling toward the bottom of the sea.

I cried out, "Save me, God!"

"I am with you. You are not alone," he replied.

Water engulfed my entire being. The unrelenting sound of gusty winds and choppy waters vanished. In the silence, I could only hear my heartbeat as I felt myself slipping away, drowning. I was sure this was the end.

I cried out to God, "Lord! Lord! You said you would be with me!"

He responded, "I am with you now. Charla, breathe!"

But as I tried to hold my breath, panic set in, and my body shook all the more uncontrollably. The pressure of the grave began to choke me. I thought, *I am going to die*, and my last breath was inhaling water. I tried to scream, "Jesus! I'm drowning! Save me!"

God calmly replied, "Breathe." He repeated it over and over again.

Franticly, I thought, *I can't breathe in water, Lord! I can't breathe in water!* I tried to remind him I was not a fish.

Again, God said, "Breathe, Charla."

Finally, I just humbled myself, trusted him, and said, "This is it. I am dying, God. But I will trust you, Lord." I closed my eyes.

God responded, "Good, that's what I needed to hear from you. Breathe the water into your lungs, Charla. And just die."

I took a deep breath and water flooded into my lungs. My panic slowly turned into peace. Amazingly, the water gave me life and hadn't killed me. I was breathing water, and I was still alive. Each time I had this dream, it always ended just before I was about to die. I always woke sweating and gasping for air. This dream felt so real, but all I needed to do was breathe in the water and trust God.

Finally, when I shifted my thinking to just trust God and listen to him, to Shema him. I seemed to cross over by faith to personally trust his thoughts for me.

When I told Joseph about the dream, we both held on to each other and cried. He said, "Deep calls out to deep, honey."

This was an intense moment for the both of us; you could hear a pin drop. In our silence, God was speaking loud and clear.

The Rauch HaKodesh gave us revelation over the years, and he was saying that we were going to experience a transition in ministry from land to sea and that it wouldn't be easy. We would experience pain. The big question, though, was what stage we were at within the dream. Prophetically, our call would be enlarged, not only to minster on land but as far and wide as the ocean stretched. We were about to experience a metamorphosis of land-to-water, divinely forged through our trials. We had many personal trials, but sadly, they came to us in the form of religious persecution and abuse from the church we were ministering in. No one wants to talk about these things, but we must.

It didn't start out that way. The abuse started when we decided to go all out for God, serving in ministry. We adapted a lifestyle of serving, no matter what we were going through. We desired more of God and would do whatever was required to do all the church asked of us. To be fair, we wanted to prove not only to others but to ourselves that we had what it took to be successful in ministry. We were young and our intentions were to encourage others, especially children, in the Lord.

Metamorphosis: Spiritual Transformation Is Painful

In Hawaii, we had a natural tendency to always serve our elders or help in anyway, no matter the cost. Eventually, we became so busy serving in ministry, we went in a downward spiral, just like my dream.

As anxious, novice Christians, we were taken by surprise by the sneaky way the enemy waits to destroy God's people. We not only witnessed poor church ethics but participated in these as well. We gravitated to the nice pats on our backs and the great compliments that helped build our ego that crept in, making us stumble and fall.

It was a learning curve for sure. If we had to do it all over again, I think I would have more confidence and godly wisdom under my belt to better navigate our situation and just speak up and make things right, but we were young and vulnerable.

I am sharing our story with you because this is how we became who we are today. These trials made a big impact on our lives. Many pastors and leaders do not listen to the deep cries of their congregation because they are too busy serving in many directions. It is bound to happen. Pastors and leaders can't please everyone; they just need to learn from mistakes and keep going. From experience, we need to be relentless in understanding and make things right. Unfortunately, this did not happen with us until it was too late. However, even in that, God made a way to use what the enemy meant for harm and turned it into his glory.

Did we forgive them? Yes, but it took time. When we did, we began to gain more wisdom and understanding in this area with other churches. By the time we were called to the next church, we flowed right into mediating between pastors and hurt parishioners to help the healing process for both parties. We didn't look for that opportunity; it looked for us. God had told us earlier that as we helped other churches, we should look for opportunities to help them forgive one another.

I am not writing this so you can bash other churches or argue with your pastor or leadership team how you feel you have been wronged. Both parties are responsible for how other Christians are caught up in this treatment. We are human. However, the pastor and the leadership team are fully responsible to make it their priority to love, teach, and encourage the spiritual growth of the members. The people come to you, and God trusts you to properly care for them.

I was really struggling to write about our true challenges concerning our metamorphosis. However, I was reminded this was my testimony.

Our Story

We came from a small island and were part of the Catholic congregation, which held Holy-Ghost–filled, charismatic prayer meetings almost every week. We simply thought that church ethics were love. We used to sing a song called "They Will Know We Are Christians by our Love." I can't speak for all Catholic churches as maybe just our small community knew how to work together to get things done. Our adoration and respect for people in general was a big part of our lives, or maybe it was just our culture of treating others with integrity (aloha) and respect, because that's how we were raised in our family.

I was introduced to my husband, Joseph, in 1989, and it was like a scene from a movie. We didn't start out like a normal couple, but we both discovered we loved the Lord with a passion but had a lot to learn. Our trials started when we first met, so our ambition to be liked or accepted in church was part of our downfall, because we both endured rejection all our lives. Hardship and pain were not new to Joseph and me, He was looking for new beginnings as well. We both came with our own set of spiritual and emotional baggage.

I cannot even recall being present at my high school graduation. It felt like a dream. My body was there, but my mind was far away. It was supposed to be one of the most celebrated times in a person's life, but it was the complete opposite. I had just found out I was pregnant. I was ashamed, and scared because I represented our church community. I was eighteen years old, walking down the aisle to receive my diploma. My friends were happy and excited but knew something was wrong with me. I shrugged them off by saying I wasn't feeling well. I could not enjoy the moment.

Three months prior, a mutual friend introduced me to Joseph. He was older, and during our first encounter, he threw up right in front of me. He was extremely drunk. I was totally disgusted, but I couldn't help being so attracted to this Hawaiian man. Our friends thought that since Joseph played the ukulele and I could hold a tune that we could provide weekly entertainment at their hangouts.

Since I was always at church with my parents, I dragged Joseph along, and Dad recruited him to play for the choir. Joseph would come to practice stoned. Dad knew he was smoking, but his heart was for Joseph to be welcomed, no matter his actions.

Once I found out I was pregnant, I had to forfeit a scholarship and face my parents, peers, and the church. My mom and dad were so upset with us; we both felt as if we let them down. This attitude applied to many of our upcoming life situations. We often felt as if we had something to prove, not only to them but to ourselves. It was a heavy humbling.

I was well-known in our small community and was featured in magazines, news articles, and interviews, on our local news station. The year prior, I won the title of Miss National Teenager Congeniality Pageant held at the Turtle Bay Hilton on Oahu. I had a statewide voice, a voice that was now tarnished.

So Joseph and I were trying to find ourselves, and the church became away to reinvent ourselves as a couple and not individuals.

After I gave birth, Joseph and I eventually got married, and we decide to serve in ministry alongside my parents. Our youth group was huge, so we helped in any way we could. We held a weekly gathering to meet up for worship and teach Bible lessons to the youth, which was filled with divine appointments. The Rauch HaKodesh would fall on all of us in a tremendous way. This helped us know how to sit in the throne room of God. This knowledge helped us when our trials intensified over the years.

In 1998, my parents were called to move to Las Vegas Nevada, and my family, including my siblings, felt we needed to follow. Once there, we were led to leave the Catholic church and join a non-denominational Christian fellowship.

In 2000 we joined a church that was growing really fast. Joseph and I decided to pioneer a trail on our own without my parents and gravitated toward the children's ministry to lead them in worship. The children's pastor gave us room to learn and grow with the program. Many times, instead of worshipping for only thirty minutes, we were given free rein to allow the Rauch HaKodesh do whatever he wanted to do within the children's service.

God brought together a cohesive and divinely appointed team, so children's church was thriving. While serving, Joseph envisioned that the children's church should have their own worship team with musicians and singers. Joseph and I started the team, and later we began to help it grow. We needed a bass player, so he recruited our oldest son, Austin, who was just ten at the time. Soon more musicians and singers joined in. Joseph spent quality time teaching this young group everything musical from keys to dynamics. He also tried to implement spontaneous worship-the prophetic so that they would be able to flow when the Holy Spirit would want to shift directions within the worship service and prayer. He made time early before church began to meet with these young worshippers, this went on for an entire year. These kids grew close to each other and loved every minute of it. Many of the youth spent weekends at my house, just worshipping with us, which was great for them to learn to assemble.

Some leaders heard about the great things happening in children's church, so we were invited to play one song in the main sanctuary for the parents and adults. Joseph prepared two songs with the youth. We had an eight-year-old on drums, and eleven-year-old on the keyboards, a seven-year-old on the bass, and Austin on the violin. Our singers ranged in age, from six to thirteen. We worked with them to have a heart of worship and to lead others to the throne room of God.

Colliding Paths / March of 2001

In 1960, two airplanes collided over New York City, killing 134 people in the air and on the ground.[7] The pilot miscalculated his location and directly ran into an oncoming plane. Just like those planes, Joseph and I were on a path to a spiritual mid-air collision, which took us by surprise.

Many times, you don't think about the overall picture in a situation. Normally, we just see our own perspectives from our point of view. If we take the time to understand this, we would prevent many unnecessary hurts and accidents of the heart and minimize collisions with others in church ministry.

It was a day to remember. The pastor called up the children, who skillfully played one song, and the church went wild in amazement as these young kids led the adults in praise. It was so good, the pastor asked if we could lead another song.

We were on a spiritual high as the kids felt approved by the adults. Joseph and I also felt as if we were righting the wrongs of our past when we started out as a young couple pregnant out of wedlock. Other pastors, our leaders, and peers were giving us great feedback. Many parents continued to compliment us, but after a couple of days, some pastors and leaders weren't happy with our accomplishments. In fact, some treated us with contempt. It felt like we were David as others were Michal, as you will see in this scripture below.

> But as the Ark of the Lord entered the City of David, Michal, the daughter of Saul, looked down from her window. When she saw King David *leaping and dancing before* the Lord, she was filled with *contempt* for him. They brought the Ark of the Lord and set it in its place inside the special tent David had prepared for it. And David sacrificed burnt offerings and peace offerings to the Lord. When he had finished his sacrifices, David blessed the people in the name of the Lord of Heaven's Armies. Then he gave to every Israelite man and woman in the crowd a loaf of bread, a cake of dates, and a cake of raisins. Then all the people returned to their homes. (2 Samuel 6:16–19, emphasis added)

We began to sense a turning of the tides, Contempt seemed to find its way to us. We could not understand it; we tried to ignore it and kept focusing on the ministry, but we could feel the awkwardness in the air. We questioned ourselves. Were we puffed up? We didn't know what happened? Why did it feel like a Michal spirit was over us.

The next week, just Joseph and I were scheduled to do a worship song in the main sanctuary. We wanted to cancel, but since we made a commitment, we pushed forward. To be honest, with the way I was feeling we should have canceled. Halfway into the song, I had a vision from the Holy Spirit. My heart already had issues which I did not understand at the time. My filter was distorted. I laugh about it today, but to be honest, the vision was quite morbid. I saw a dead body being embalmed while I was worshiping, I decided to share it with the entire congregation. Yes, prophetically, this was a pretty deep revelation, but the church was still new to the prophetic. In addition, I should have asked permission to share, it because it was understood wrong.

From there, things went from bad to worse. We received great compliments from the congregation, concerning our song, but many pastors and leaders ignored us. Spiritually, we could feel something was not right. To say that my dream was coming into play was an understatement.

Thereafter I dreamed that certain pastors were talking about us. I denied it because it was crazy to even think this. But I could feel rumors spreading in my gut, and leaders could not look us in our eyes. I spent countless nights asking the Lord, "Is this you showing me? How do we handle this?" So we retreated back to the only way we knew to handle it: worshipping in our home with our kids. Then, the unthinkable happened. Innocent children, those we ministered to, casually mentioned what their parents were saying about us. Gossip, slander, and hateful words were shared to us in secret. Those parents were the leaders and pastors of the church. We were so shocked and hurt. I hated to hear more.

But the youth loved us so much, they told us more than we could handle. I often went home crying after services but held in the pain. Our hearts were broken at the lies and gossip that spread by pastors and leaders. How could this be? To our faces, they were so nice, but behind our backs, we were carelessly judged.

The stress mounted feeling something bad was about to happen. Sure enough, the children's pastor met with us and told us that they were bringing in a new worship pastor who would teach the youth how to worship. They wanted him to oversee the entire worship team and create a choir. But we were already the worship pastors for the children's church, so this did not make sense to us. In fact, we were shocked. It was as if the rug were being pulled out right from under us. To be honest, it felt like a foreclosure on a farmer and his land.

We didn't take that lying down but retaliated, became angry and offended, and felt rejected, shut down. We were demoted.

Many things happened after that, one right after another. We questioned the church and its leadership. We tried to speak with the senior pastor, but he was too busy for us. We began to study the Word of God harder than ever before and tried to understand our role as parishioners and as leaders.

In the meantime, our kids were tossed back and forth by these events as we frankly talked about all the yuckiness we were going through. We decided it was time to take a break, but we had one more ministry event that we had to do with the kids' worship team.

We were invited to play worship at one of the affiliate churches off campus. We needed to drive the kids over to the event. But Joseph's license had been suspended a week earlier because we could not afford car insurance. That morning, I didn't feel comfortable driving a big van full of kids, so Joseph decided to drive. We didn't get stopped by the police or anything like that it was just the thought that we were not holding true to our integrity. Our day was moving so fast the enemy had a way to use this against us. Since we were ripe for an attack with our prior situation. I thought I could handle the van, but I couldn't, and it was too late to find a sub for us. With all that was going on already, we helped speed up the process of my dream as it became a reality in our lives.

That night when we got home, Joseph felt that we should tell the children's pastor what happened. But before we could, someone had already talked to the leadership team, that Joseph drove without his license. Sure enough, the next day, we were summoned to the pastor's office as if we were kids in trouble ready to be expelled. After this, we began to experience serious rejection from the church.

We were cut from the ministry and decide not to fight it because we knew we were in the wrong, so we just took our punishment of driving a van full of church members kids which Joseph's had no license.

We wanted to take a break but not like this. To add to our shame, they put my older brother in charge of where we had fallen short. If removing us from our position were not hurtful enough, this was the most painful.

Joseph, I, and the kids were all devastated. We still went to church and sat in the back. If we did sit in the front, we were ignored, or others pretended with fake smiles. Everyone knew we were being disciplined. We were drowning, definitely like my dream. It felt as if we had to do the walk of shame every Sunday just to reach our seats. We could not take the rejection any longer. The next Sunday, we hid in our home and decided not to go to church. The following Sunday, we finally decided we needed to find some sort of healing to help us through this trial.

We decided to visit another church in the area, but strangely enough, they weren't very welcoming. We couldn't figure out why, so we tried still another church the next week. The same thing happened; we weren't welcome. We felt even worse, so lost that we went right back to worshipping at home alone with our kids.

The next week, my younger brother called me, and said I wouldn't believe what his close friend from another church received in their email. A letter had been sent out to all the churches in the area, warning them not to welcome Joe and Charla, who had left the church in offense and were wolves in sheep's clothing. The letter concluded with a request that we not be allowed to serve! "There are six things the Lord *hates*, seven that are detestable to him: haughty eyes, a *lying tongue*, hands that shed innocent blood, a heart that *devises wicked schemes*, feet that are quick to rush into evil, *a false witness who pours out lie and a person who stirs up conflict in the community"* (Proverbs 6:16–19, emphasis added).

We felt destroyed! We couldn't believe it. At this point, we needed to make the situation right. We were so angry and hurt. We confronted different pastors, and they were shocked and denied they sent out a letter. We tried to meet up with the senior pastor again, but he was not available. They sent other pastors to soothe us over, hoping the problem would just go away. Finally, the children's pastor met with us and was in disbelief at what had taken place. She tried to comfort us and get to the bottom of what happened, but we were so hurt. We just wanted to clear our names and move on. Scripture reassured us: "A good name is more desirable than great riches; to be esteemed is better than silver or gold" (Proverbs 22:1).

As Christians, we are not to spread lies and gossip about others, especially when we don't know them personally.

As we now reflect on what happened, we believed the enemy meant to destroy us and our church family. The enemy wanted to divide us, and believe me, he did. We became conscious and overly observant at what was happening constantly. We asked God to help us navigate this process because our critical attitudes grew worse. This was our metamorphosis. But we stayed stuck in that pain without healing. We stayed at this church for eight years trying to regain hope in leadership and fellowship. Even floating from church to church at times.

Even so, this brokenness seemed to unlock spiritual keys that maximized our capacity to hear God's voice in our struggles. Our communication with the Holy Spirit became a cherished lifestyle. Because of this trial, we learned to understand perspectives and realized that each pastor and leader is human and would fail us, but God never would.

Church Ethics

When a believer first comes to Christ, they are so happy to learn all about the new Christian life that they will experience with their new church family. They feel accepted and are willing to do anything to be a part of it. As a new believer, they begin to exercise their newfound faith and put full trust in the leaders that have been assigned to them, not by the church but by God. Their confession is a public demonstration of the new life they are about to embark on.

Soon, they will want to be part of God's kingdom and help grow as part of the church. Manipulation and religious abuse are inevitable. But just like any family, we are made to grow together no matter the hardship, the pain, and the victories. That is what family is all about. The church needs to be a safe place to make mistakes but still carry on and learn together-family. No matter the shortcomings, that person won't leave because they know they are family and they stick together. This kind of relationship only grows stronger and stronger. If not, the enemy will sneak his way in between all miscommunication.

Many large churches may lack cultivating a secure family atmosphere. Not everyone can be pastors. We can have a pastor's heart but not the maturity of running a spiritual house. Many believers who serve in ministry may be in the wrong ministry because they may have the heart but lack perseverance due to inexperience. We can gain understanding and godly wisdom as found in the following passage.

> Listen, my sons, to a father's instruction; pay attention and *gain understanding*. I give you sound learning, so do not forsake my teaching. For I too was a son to my father, still tender, and cherished by my mother. Then he taught me, and he said to me, "Take hold of my words with all your heart; keep my commands, and you will live. *Get wisdom, get understanding*; do not forget my words or turn away from them. Do not forsake wisdom, and she will protect you; love her, and she will watch over you. The beginning of wisdom is this: Get wisdom. *Though it cost all you have*, get understanding. Cherish her, and she will exalt you; embrace her, and she will honor you. She will give you a garland to grace your head and present you with a glorious crown." Listen, my son, accept what I say, and the *years of your life will be many. I instruct you* in the way of wisdom and lead you *along straight paths. When you walk, your steps will not be hampered; when you run, you will not stumble.* Hold on to instruction, do not let it go; guard it well, for it is your life. Do not set foot on *the path of the wicked* or walk in the way of evildoers. Avoid it, *do not travel on it*; turn from it and go on your way. For they cannot rest until they do evil; they are robbed of sleep till they make someone stumble. They eat the bread of wickedness and drink the wine of violence …Give careful thought to *the paths for your feet* and be steadfast in all your ways. Do not turn to the right or the left; keep your foot from evil. (Proverbs 4:1–17, 26–27, emphasis added)

Once you pledge to get wisdom at any cost, it will run its course in your life. Salvation is free because Jesus paid the price in so many areas of our lives, but a personal anointing costs something: perseverance through your trials. Why do we need our own anointing? Because that anointing breaks the yoke of our personal bondages, and we can then help others in those same areas.

In the church family, we are all on different paths, on different timelines of growth and experiences. Many churches and their assemblies lack this understanding. If I knew now what I should've known back then, I would have been able to understand and process what happened to us in a more peaceful way. Also, if the church leaders and pastors had known this, they would have handled the situation entirely different. We are all on different paths and timelines. This is where the enemy waits to attack us and cause havoc.

The word "path" appears in fifty-six Bible verses, so I think it's safe to say we are on a path of life. A path is a way beaten, formed, or trodden by the feet of persons or animals that have already been there before. We can be assured that God is with us on our path. "I look behind me and you're there, then up ahead and you're there, too—your reassuring presence, coming and going" (Psalm 139:5 MSG). We are all on a path, different journeys at different times. This Scripture has been used many times to say that the Lord will find you no matter what stage you are at on your faith journey. You cannot hide from him; in fact, nothing can separate him from you.

As mature Christians, we need to recognize the people that are in our lives are either ahead of us or behind us. If they are ahead, we must respect their wisdom and give them a chance to teach us. If they are behind us, we give them the grace and patience to catch up with us, because we have already passed that way. In fact, we have blazed a trail for them. "But I'll take the hand of those who don't know the way, who can't see where they're going. I'll be a personal guide to them, directing them through unknown country. I'll be right there to show them what roads to take, make sure they don't fall into the ditch. These are the things I'll be doing for them —sticking with them, not leaving them for a minute" (Isaiah 42:16 MSG).

At the time when we were going through our own metamorphosis, all the parties were on different paths.

When reading about King David and his life journey in the Bible, the Lord revealed to us through our metamorphosis with the church leaders and pastors that we were on a different timeline on our spiritual journey. In 2 Samuel 6:17, when David was dancing before the ark of the covenant, he had not a care in the world. David's only focus was the Lord, and he didn't care how he looked. In fact, he danced so hard his clothes fell off, exposing him. In the same way, Joseph and I exposed ourselves, so much so that, to some, it was an offense and not a celebration just as Michal was so offended.

Joseph and I felt just like David dancing in front of the ark. We enjoyed the dance before the Lord with the children's worship team on that platform that day. However, at the same time, from the perspective of the children's pastor, she could have been in a season like Samuel the prophet, looking for that one person to anoint while David was out in the fields. Now, from the perspective of the new choir director coming in to take over the children's choir, he could have been in a season ready to sing over King Saul to get rid of those evil spirits that haunted him. Each of us is on different paths, different seasons of our spiritual journey with different timelines that caused a mid-air collision. This collision gave the enemy time to work on all of us. Thank God, over the years, he has given us the opportunity to make things right and forgive each other and move forward.

Who knows? Maybe the new choir director was given the opportunity to take the ministry to new levels, and he was in a season of being King David dancing in front of the ark. Maybe Joseph and I were spiritual Michals who were filled with contempt. We might not know what area or season we are in, but we must be able to recognize how the enemy works. We must understand our journey, especially in fellowship with the body of Christ. That spirit of Michal is sneaking up on in the church and running rampant in our hearts. But this should not go on any longer.

We have been from one end of the spectrum to the other concerning congregations and proper church etiquette because we experienced it. We just had a hard time being healed from it after all was said and done, but we choose to learn from it. Because of this experience, we decided to search the Scriptures and were led to understand on a wide scope how God was working things out for our good. So we developed discernment.

I always pray that new Christians find a church home that operates in integrity and love and that they develop true and genuine relationships with all who attend. This is why being a pastor or a leader is a calling because only God can hold you up when you feel you just can't do it anymore.

A church family is to aid them in their faith journey is critical to growing into a healthy Christian lifestyle that can be passed down from generation to generation. A relationship between a church and your family has to be strong enough to allow for mistakes, growth, and imperfections. You can move forward, knowing that one member is not higher than the other, but you can have the attitude that we are in it together.

With that said, you are forming godly friendships by teaching each other how to walk together in faith. When you trust someone, they open up a door to be teachable. When you are teachable, it encourages healthy growth.

It seems rare these days to find congregations that offer simple fellowship and contend for strong biblical truths and practice what they teach. No matter what church you attend, you will experience some sort of growth pains. Some people are called to be in the church, and some are called to be fully functional outside the church. We all have to balance this out.

Joseph and I learned, when we finally left that church, in order to survive our metamorphosis, we needed to forgive ourselves and those who hurt us. We can do stupid things when we want what we want, which is why we need each other to help through the process.

There is a common saying: "The grass isn't always greener on the other side of the fence." This is true because there is no grass to begin with. It's time to start tilling your own soil and farm the spiritual land that God has for you to grow.

Joseph and I believe that God allowed all we experienced. He needed to humble us so that we understood that we didn't own any ministry. Because of my character and where we came from in our genealogy, we needed to be broken to be the best people possible to serve him. What the enemy meant to harm us was to grow us. This was part of our metamorphosis. We had to see and feel all that we went through so we would never be that way toward anyone on our spiritual journey. We thought our metamorphosis was done, but we were wrong. It was just starting, and more trials came, this time, in the form of attacks on my kids.

CHAPTER 5

SUICIDE: OUR TRIAL BECOMES OUR MINISTRY

Do not forsake wisdom, and she will protect you; love her, and she will watch over you. The beginning of wisdom is this: get wisdom. Though it cost all you have, get understanding.
—Proverbs 4:6–7 NLT

IN 2004, MY eldest son ran away from home numerous times, and I felt we lost him mentally. Through the shuffle of ministry, he retaliated by not coming home for days. At sixteen, he wandered the streets of Las Vegas. He wore long black coats, painted his fingernails black, and always smelled like smoke. At first, we were very concerned; sadly, it was because we had an image to protect. We were children's pastors. What would others think if we couldn't keep our own children in line? Joseph and I felt this weight and thought we were neglecting him. I cried out for wisdom and sought relentlessly for answers on how to handle this situation.

One night, my mom and dad decided to come over and try to intervene and get through to their first grandson. We waited and waited, then finally Austin walked through our front door. He smelled like weed, and he was drinking. A fight broke out in our living room. Austin was out of control; he seemed possessed. Joseph tried to hold him down while his younger siblings retreated to their rooms. It was physically and mentally draining. Our Christian values of peaceful communication were out the window. Austin tried to run again, falling on the floor. At this point, Austin and Joseph struggled with each other.

Austin escaped Joseph's grasp and ran straight toward the front door where my dad grabbed ahold of him. Both parties were crying, spitting, and yelling. Austin screamed, "I hate my life! I want to die! I hate you! And I hate the church and everything about it!" We tried to lock him in the room, but by morning, he ran away again.

Many times, Austin escaped death for sure. This went on for many years: the fight, the hurt, and his pain. It came in waves. We had no way of figuring out when these episodes would strike. We finally got involved in deliverance ministry and thought this was the answer. We studied and read about anything concerning suicide and the strongman and its stronghold from the Bible. These Christian terms refer to a process for casting spirits out of people like Jesus did. We would pray and pray, fast and fast, and even do several sessions of deliverance on my son, and nothing happened. In fact, he seemed to get worse.

We called the church elders and the pastors to pray for us. No matter what we did, it seemed to be no use, and we felt as if we were getting nowhere. At one point, I had to call the police because he pulled out a kitchen knife and threatened to kill himself if I got any closer to him. I panicked and had no answers to help him. By the time the police arrived, he was calm. They still arrested him and hospitalized him because he threatened to kill himself.

The hospital worked for some time. They diagnosed him with severe depression, and they said he might have other mental issues that needed to be checked. However, Joseph was working for the church at that time, and we had no medical insurance, so we could not cover his treatment. We tried other resources, but the timing was wrong or they were too far away.

Austin suffered from shame and rejection. We didn't want to admit it at the time, but we played a part in those feelings. We needed further assessments and assistance to even get in to see a counselor; however, we couldn't even pay for an initial fee. This was incredibly hard and challenging; it felt as if no one could help us. This led to more feelings of rejection, not only for Austin but for Joseph and me as well.

Looking back, I was in denial because I didn't think the hospital could help him as much as the church could. I just thought he needed a spirit cast out, like how Jesus cast out demons. I was wrong. I can see that now we needed both. But what else could I have done? We plunged into worship and placed our worries in God's hands. We cried out for help for Austin. We desperately needed God's wisdom.

God was silent, so my attitude started to get salty. I felt as if God had left us out to dry. Deep down, I felt I should have a perfect cookie-cutter family that modeled Jesus. I grew up seeing church families like that, so I expected that from my own family. Where were those families that were suffering like we were? I wondered how many people in church never talked about their real ugliness. Joseph and I set up beautiful parties and Christian programs for the church. Perfect families with no struggles like ours gathered together.

I was not only desperate to save my son but analyzed my own life. Had I ever felt like committing suicide or struggled with feeling rejected? God revealed the answer to me: yes. He was dealing with not only Austin but with me as well.

God had to show me that I needed to let go of the idea of a so-called perfect family. We were not perfect; we were original. I had seen other leaders and church members lead normal lives, and our trials seemed to be harder. I needed to deal with those comparisons first before I could deal with my son. The more I tried to show that we were a perfect family in church, the worse our trials became. Finally, we just stopped trying to please others and stopped putting up appearances as the perfect family serving in ministry. We were done.

All I wanted was peace for my son and for our house. We wanted to get rid of that torment of always trying to please the church leaders by doing all that they asked of us. I was afraid of being rejected and ashamed of not being perfect. I realized that was what Austin was feeling with us.

Joseph and I humbled ourselves under the mercy of God and worshiped every day. Those moments cleared our thoughts and gave us perspective. Worship was our safe place. We didn't know how to handle what we were dealing with concerning Austin. There were days our situation was okay, but the next day, a fight would break out between us. He got into trouble, and we were right back where we started. This went on for five years!

Broken and exhausted, we continued to press in to hearing from God. We believed we were on the right track. But one day as I was at home alone with only Austin while the younger kids were at school. I was washing dishes, and Austin came downstairs and stood right next to me. He leaned back on the counter and said, in a deep voice, "This is my house."

Taken aback, I turned around. That was not his voice. I looked him in the eyes. "What did you say?"

He repeated it. "This is my house."

As a spiritual intercessor, my normal reaction was to engage in full-blown spiritual warfare with this spirit. However, God's grace and mercy saved me that day because the Holy Spirit intervened. I reacted in a way I normally don't react. I was so hurt and scared for my son as this spirit was trying to take his life. Slowly, I began to hug him and felt his heart. I felt his pain, anger, and a sense of loss. I began to cry. I remembered when I gave birth to him and held him in my arms for the first time. God reminded that I was still his mother. As I continued to hold him, he tried to pull away. I began to say, "This is God's house," referring to Austin's soul, his heart.

He slowly relaxed in my arms as we both fell to the ground. I repeated, "This is God's house," and "Mommy loves you, and if you cannot fight, I will fight for you."

We both cried in each other's arms. I told him, "No matter what you do, wherever you go, or however you may feel toward me, I will never stop loving you. I forgive you, Austin, but please forgive me. I don't care about all the wrong things you have done to me or the bad things you have said, but we are not going to give up on you. I love you. You are mine, Austin, and I'm giving you back to God." At that powerful moment, God was also speaking the same things to me as his daughter.

Austin cried so hard; he began to throw up a clear white slime as the presence of the Holy Spirit hovered over us. Austin slept for two days after that incident, only getting up to eat and go to the bathroom. He played his guitar, worshiping God in his room and crying out for his help in his struggles.

I was at the end of trying to battle this spirit. I depended on the Holy Spirit to daily give me specific instructions. I was desperate and love was the key that would resolve this situation. That spirit left him that day while we were crying on the floor. Over the years, this spirit kept coming back although not to the extent that we had encountered in our kitchen that day. We had to remind ourselves to keep on depending on God's wisdom and manifest his love toward my son.

As a mother, the Holy Spirit told me I was to bridge the gap for my children. I was to hold them up in the areas where they were struggling. I was to help them grow and heal in areas they didn't understand why they were experiencing it.

My relationship with my son was like a tornado that popped up from out of nowhere. I never knew when his atmosphere would be hot or cold. He was unstable and not in control of his feelings. Instead of crying, he grew frustrated and slipped into anger. His anger controlled his mind, and negative thoughts flooded in. These thoughts brought a recurring cycle of his past failures to keep him in this mental prison. He felt as if there were no way out. Austin's mind was cluttered with negative reminders, and he felt hopeless to fix. He was physically and mentally overwhelmed, and it was choking the air out of him. The only escape that made sense to him was to end his life. But this was a lie from the enemy.

This is the hardest to write because we are revealing our true hardship. Unfortunately, my second-oldest son was now showing the same symptoms as Austin. So not only was I dealing with one child but now with two sons.

I know others out there have gone through this. Because of this illness, my sons became the lab rats while I as their mother was the doctor. On other days, I felt I was that lab rat. The rule was never to run but stay and work it out together; that was the only way we made it through. This experience revealed a root of low self-worth and rejection issues within our family's bloodline along with other negative character traits.

Now I can't give you the answers you may need concerning suicide as everyone's situation is different. But I can share my story and how God led me to seek his wisdom in dealing with my sons. You may be able to relate to what I have been through, but remember, Shema your way through it.

As an intercessor, I felt my son's struggle, and the Holy Spirit helped me understand what he was feeling. I felt defeated at times but trusted God continually. My faith level increased, and I gained wisdom and confidence in my prayers. I began to speak about my sons' future with me and our family. I started to pray for mothers and families who were experiencing the same hardships I was; my Shema was genuine. I later realized that my children had the heart of intercessors, and in that sensitivity, they felt the weight of the world, including their own. I taught them the importance of praying and separating their own burdens from the burdens of others they carried in prayer. I believe those who feel suicidal are born intercessors. If the enemy can eliminate them, he eliminates genuine compassionate intercessors that can move mountains.

You might be thinking, *Why didn't you just pray it off or cast that spirit out and be done with it?* For us, it wasn't that simple, because God wanted us to find the underlying cause. Only the Holy Spirit could show us how to do that. It took a combination of prayer, fasting, and godly wisdom to get to the bottom of where this spirit came from before it finally left my sons. It was in our DNA.

In the next chapter, we will share what we know about our personal DNA. But it took a blanket of love to keep working at this issue with my family and especially my sons. One night, we had a flare up of aggression with my second son, and the Lord told me this spirit of suicide was not only deaf but dumb. We then realized only vibrations (music and worship) could move in the areas we could not reach, so we pressed into worship and fasted. We didn't fast from food; we fasted from an impatient spirit—an impatient spirit that was on me. This spirit wants a quick deliverance, a fast fix. However, as growing believers in our faith, God will utilize every opportunity to accumulate spiritual authority especially if the enemy has anything to do with it. Through your perseverance in overseeing deliverance You as the deliverer will need to recognize that it may not happen overnight. My son needed to work on their relationship with Christ and since it was a generational thing, I needed to work on myself as well. We needed Godly wisdom to walk through this deliverance together. As Christians we want that person to be freed from those tormenting spirits so badly, we miss the mark on what God is doing. We trusted in God and his timing. The book of Mark describes this type of holy intervention:

> When Jesus saw that the people came running together, He rebuked the unclean spirit, saying to it: *"Deaf and dumb spirit, I command you, come out of him and enter him no more!"* Then the spirit cried out, convulsed him greatly, and came out of him. And he became as one dead, so that many said, "He is dead." But Jesus took him by the hand and lifted him up, and he arose. And when He had come into the house, His disciples asked Him privately, "Why could we not cast it out?" So, He said to them, *"This kind can come out by nothing but prayer and fasting.* (Mark 9:25–29 NKJV, emphasis added)

The Bible speaks of a spiritual realm that takes prayer and fasting to conquer what we truly don't understand. Daniel knew it. Paul knew it, and of course, Jesus knew it. You must know it as well and be able to discern the spirits as noted in 1 Corinthians 12:10: "And to another the effecting of miracles, and to another prophecy, and to another the distinguishing of spirits, to another various kinds of tongues, and to another the interpretation of tongues" (NASB). The Lord will teach you discernment. Psalms 119:66 says: "Teach me good discernment and knowledge, for I believe in Your commandments" (NASB).

We weren't dealing with a spirit that somehow hopped on us by opening a sinful door, although that is possible. Instead, we were dealing with a spirit that had been in our family from generation to generation. As I understood this, the Lord God allowed me to feel what my boys felt. Since

I was an intercessor, God granted my request. However, I didn't realize that I was feeling what they were feeling. These feelings overwhelmed me one morning. First, I felt totally alone. I began to go into a deep depression I wondered what was wrong as I had nothing to be depressed about.

As the day went on, I became overwhelmed with bills and small issues around the house. The more I thought about it, the worse the problems seemed. Cleaning, washing clothes, and even taking a bath felt depressing.

Joe came home from work and wondered why I felt that way. He didn't know what was happening to me. I began to cry and cry and felt yucky about myself, so I reflected on past accomplishments. The depression cloud grew thicker. I felt so unloved, so forgotten. I felt like a total failure. The lies piled up as I walked down this negative road.

I reached out in prayer. "Lord, I'm afraid. I can't feel you. Where are you?" I held on to prayer for a couple of days. I was an emotional wreck, and God didn't answer me at first.

Finally, on the third day God answered me. My iPhone chimed in from Facebook. A church located in Redding, California, shared a video of their worship team singing a song called "God of Miracles." The song was to God from a father who lost his child. The father told God that even in the hardest of moments of losing his son, he still believed God was a God of miracles.

However, my revelation came in a different way. God was responding to me, saying that he "believed in me" because he is the God of miracles. So touched, I felt God holding me. Listening to that song brought me deliverance in some way. I wanted to release those feelings. My relationship with Jesus and the prompting of the Holy Spirit were strongly rooted in me, which gave me the push or power to get that spirit off me. However, others may not have that relationship, that direction. They may not have family members to support them and patiently walk through that process with them. I believe that is how the devil has been stealing lives from those he can.

All emotions of negativity left me, and in a millisecond, the Lord reminded me that I needed to demonstrate love to my boys. The way I was feeling is how they felt every day with that spirit of suicide. In my conversations with them, they shared feelings of regret, regret so deep that they were too young to have accumulated. They carried so much on their shoulders—it was mind-blowing. Again, the Lord told me to just love them through it, yes, just love them through it. Teach them to just yearn for God's presence. That is God's unconditional love.

I have spent twenty years learning to love my sons through many situations and being obedient in hearing and obeying God through it all. To Shema him. Remember, at the beginning of the book, I talked about the different aspects of the Shema. One aspect means to "hear and obey" coming from God. However, the Shema I'm talking about in this situation was from me to God, crying out to him to "hear and act on my behalf"—for my boys, my children.

Today my sons are well and healed. We are always learning as we walk through this journey together. God's wisdom, knowledge, and understanding helped, but the key was to love them through this season. It was a process and still is. But love is patient and takes time. When my son was on the floor in the kitchen, God saw my love and compassion for my son and gave us the victory to overcome that spirit that day. Love is a powerful weapon to cover your children; it can break demonic spirits off anyone. A warfare or fighting prayer did not save us, but we were saved when I humbled myself in positioning my heart to love them through it. At times, I almost felt as if I were ignoring their flare ups, but in God's kingdom, we had confidence in the faith that he gave us to have a victory. I will share more about the positioning of your heart in the coming chapters.

CHAPTER 6

ANCESTRAL DNA: CHANGE THE CYCLE

For I will cleanse their blood that I have not cleansed: for the Lord dwelleth in Zion.
—Joel 3:21 KJV

IN THE BOOK of Joel, the prophet states that genuine change will bring restoration and the divine intervention of God's presence to cleanse the blood of your enemies. This was a big revelation because God was showing me that the enemy was ourselves. We need to cleanse ourselves and the sins of our fathers from our ancestors, our bloodline.

I am sure my grandpa and grandma behaved unjustly in their lifetime. In fact, I think that in my lifetime, our family lineage participated in sinful behaviors that we are probably paying for today. Do you ever wonder why some have it harder than others? I believe this is why. We not only reap of the blessings from our past but also the negatives. Our DNA recycles because that is the nature of DNA. DNA will replicate its cycle in every season of your life and your lineage until you take the opportunity to recreate it for the better.

Your DNA will constantly regenerate the way it has every day until you recognize its cycles. Once you recognize these in your life or in your children's lives, you can create a new pattern to replace the old one. So if you seem to have a bad mishap on a certain day each and every year or if a certain situation seems to regularly replay, your blood from your lineage is repeating itself. Maybe you are repeating a relative's cycle or pattern which would just gravitate to you until you change that pattern.

Social media aided us in confirming that, each year in my family, we had famine months—months with a lack of food and financial strain. (Thanks, Facebook memories!) This was always during June, July, and August when the children were off school. Facebook shared these memories, and the Lord showed me we needed to change that cycle. So we did by creating new and wiser choices and turned those months into a successful season. We saved and made sure that this time around, we had money for a vacation or at least money for the children to get school supplies and new clothes. It took time to recognize the negative patterns and make these changes. The worst was always Mother's Day when I was traumatized.

Every year, my husband and I got into a small fight that escalated, and the entire house was affected. But one year, my second-oldest son ran away on Mother's Day, and we didn't see him for a month. We called the police and searched for him everywhere. When he turned up, a crowd of boys had beaten him and left him for dead. By God's grace and mercy, he was alive and brought home to recover after the hospital. Every year after that, I was a little scared that a big fight would break out on Mother's Day. We recognized that and made an intentional and conscious effort each year to not let my Mother's Day be destroyed by the enemy.

My Ancestral DNA

In hindsight, I've had a very hard time with academics. I struggled with reading comprehension and took a while to understand what I read. I had to reread the same material several times to really understand the entire paragraph or even a sentence. Math was the worse. It just looked like a bunch of chaotic nonsense on the page and gave me anxiety and made me extremely aggravated. I gravitated to hands-on lessons to navigate through school. I became determined to learn, and everything was ten times harder for me than for everyone else in my class. Even in that I was barely making the grade.

In Hawaii, my teachers sadly weren't familiar with the differences in the learning disabilities and placed me in a Special Ed class that tried to help. But I felt embarrassed and dumber than I already felt. I was definitely a very slow learner and a late bloomer, never knowing I had learning disabilities. In time, I taught myself other ways to make my learning easier. I did not know this learning disability would be passed on to my children, and spiritual matters passed down to them as well.

With reflection, God showed me the natural abilities—abilities to be intuitive or very sensitive to the supernatural things around me—in my family lineage. I naturally saw things in the supernatural as normal. I had visions, dreams, and other supernatural sensations while growing up but never understood them. My personal relationship with the Lord showed me to ask for wisdom and humble myself in this and learn about this gift, and he began to show me things.

I wondered how I acquired this gift, and I began to ask my mom questions. She told me we have always had the gift of being sensitive in the supernatural in our bloodline. My mom said, however, she didn't know if my ancestors inquired of God for the main source of their revelation or guidance, but they participated in this strong practice. In the natural world, this would be considered a witch, medium, sorcerer, fortune teller, necromancer, or reader of omens. I struggled with this and was afraid because I had felt I dabbled in this at some point. I asked the Lord to show me how to get rid of this evil lineage. God led me to repent for my family lineage and for learning information from dark places. God even revealed to me how my relatives would conjure up ancestors to seek information and build in-home shrines to offer up their gifts to these dead individuals as part of witchcraft. I had to always question and make sure that I was receiving a heavenly download from the Lord himself, and if it wasn't, I would ignore it.

I didn't want any part of this gift, it scared me but God said, "You were born with this gift, so you need to utilize it for me. If you allow me to teach you how to skillfully use it, I will show you." The fine line is to always question or discern the source of information.

He showed me John 4:1: "Beloved, believe not every spirit, but try the spirits whether they are of God: because many false prophets are gone out into the world" (KJV). God told me that if I use that gift and allow him to reveal these secrets and mysteries, I would be able to navigate what he wants me to use it for. However, if I misused this gift for my own agenda, my revelations would be distorted because it would come from a dark place. God told me if I sought information from anywhere other than from his presence or guidance, I would be trusting the demonic. This sorcery and practices of divination would open a door to witchcraft, medium, sorceries, foretellers, necromancers, or readers of omens to operate not only in my life but in the lives of my family members as well. So I was very careful to always stay in the guidelines that God had given me to use these gifts and did not try to use God for my own agenda. God always became the source to reveal mysteries, secrets, knowledge, and insights to Joseph and me so that we could help not only ourselves but others.

I totally understood what God was saying, because this was called the prophetic—or being sensitive to God. We do not conjure up the dead, or cast spells, and all that divination stuff—in the Christian faith. In other words, we don't participate or dabble in that but focus in the gifts of the Holy Spirit. What is the prophetic? Romans 12:6 refers to prophecy as one of the spiritual gifts given by the indwelling of the Holy Spirit. The gift of prophecy is a supernatural ability to receive and convey messages from God. It should edify, exhort, and comfort those who participate in it. These messages come from God and God alone. The Bible refers to this very thing in the book of Daniel:

> Daniel answered the king and said, "No wise men, enchanters, magicians, or astrologers can show to the king the mystery that the king has asked, but there is a God in heaven who reveals

mysteries, and he has made known to King Nebuchadnezzar what will be in the latter days. Your dream and the visions of your head as you lay in bed are these: To you, O king, as you lay in bed came thoughts of what would be after this, and he who reveals mysteries made known to you what is to be. But as for me, this mystery has been revealed to me, not because of any wisdom that I have more than all the living, but in order that the interpretation may be made known to the king, and that you may know the thoughts of your mind. (Daniel 2:27–30 ESV)

This ability runs through my bloodline from my mom, her mom, and back several generations. Although I was born with this ability, it needed to be filtered. That processor was the fire of God. And the fire of God was my trials. God had to break me to get me to Shema.

God needed to govern everything that I would receive in the supernatural. If he did not, I would risk learning from evil sources governed by the enemy. Again, I would be labeled as a modern-day psychic, witch, magician, sorcerer, shaman, healer, medicine woman, or with a similar title. But this, I was not. I am just like you, a lover of God's presence and a passionate student of his wisdom, born with this gift. In seeking him for that wisdom, other gifts followed that added to my personal relationship with Jesus.

When I was born, God knew that one day, I would have to relinquish this gift to him. My trials were a testing ground to see if I could carry the responsibility or the weight of what he would share with me for others, but I had to learn to do it with my children first.

I went through a spiritual training from the Holy Spirit. This was a specific detailed program designed for me and our lineage because their bloodline still flowed in our veins. Character traits, both good and bad, had transferred from one generation to the next, which was our legacy.

Each of us has tormenting repetitive cycles of bad habits that can cause mental pain and trauma. These experiences are grafted into our family lineage, passed down from generation to generation. we were dealing with some of these attitudes from our sons. In addition to rejection, stress, and trauma, the spirit of suicide was passed down and was always looming over our heads. I wondered where it came from. The Lord told me first it came from a selfish spirit. This spirit wants what it wants, no matter the cost, and if it does not get it, it would then threaten suicide to hurt those around them. Secondly, this attitude will continue to make you look down on yourself. Your mind is on a constant loop of negative messages, saying you are a nobody and have no sense of self-worth. You're always looking back to past failures so that you feel there is no way out of this prison and the best way to escape is to end your life.

We uncovered this underlying rejection through ancestral experiences. We had the responsibility to stand and make a change in our heritage moving forward. The secrets God revealed to me were pivotal in changing our bloodline. Again, I'll say it once more. I had to ask forgiveness from our family lineage. I also had to ask God for mercy in what I didn't understand.

These issues are in our blood, which gives life to our brains, so they are mental disorders. Our genetic codes determine our blood lines. These spirits will sneak in through family failures from our past ancestors. God will help you recognize habits, emotions, and attitudes and take responsibility to change what is keeping you from healthy growth in your life. We can establish a new cycle.

Research shows that negative habits and a repetitive cycle passes down from one generation to the next. These scientists tested mice to see if heredity can transfer from one generation to the next. Their finds were amazing. We know that disease and sickness can transfer through bone and blood, but we don't talk much about the emotional or spiritual traits of positive and bad habits, which are passed down as well. To confirm how powerful DNA transference is, these scientists placed a male and a female mouse in a maze every day for a week. The mice started out slowly but quickly reached the end of the maze to collect their pieces of cheese and peanut butter. Each time, they got faster and faster.

They then mated the mice. When their babies were born, they placed each baby in this same maze their parents had gone through. Each baby was separately placed in this maze, and without hesitation and with no previous exposure to the maze, each of them knew exactly where they needed to go. Their parents' skill was passed on to them and just kicked in. It was already in their blood. Now if that is transferable, so are bad habits as well.

These baby mice did not have to even work hard to figure out this maze. They received the blessings of hard work from their parents, when it took their parents weeks to accomplish it. They even placed the baby mice back in the maze without peanut butter, and they still navigated it with ease.

Our children showed definite signs of receiving the transferable skills which Joseph and I worked hard to learn. We also were dealing with generational trauma, tragedy, shame, and depression that was linked to our ancestral bloodline from both sides.

For some of you, God will lead you to understand something different to handle suicide. We are all different, so we have to take the time to go to God and listen to specific instructions from him as to how to handle it. We knew our children's neurological pathways weren't functioning properly to bring peaceful resolutions in times of distress; they constantly acted out in negative ways. We felt blessed if we got through one day without any of them aggressively breaking out in anger or in a meltdown of depression that invited that suicidal spirit to inhabit them. This was ancestral transference of our DNA. We knew we had a transfer of music skills on both sides of the family. The Holy Spirit led us to use that to our advantage, which was why worship played a major role in our house. However, we were healed, but our kids were dealing with past church experiences. So getting them to worship together was not easy. They still blamed the church for their issues. All our kids could play an instrument and sing, but we really struggled to even sing one worship song together since our kids were in their teens now and we weren't regular church goers. However, we had an inherited ancestral anointing from the Holy Spirit for worship, which changed the atmosphere, and one song could cradle us in God's covering together for months.

God will give you the secret for your family. We tried to do a hard-core deliverance and prayer meeting with our second child. But his issues grew worse, so we knew God was definitely teaching us not to battle or engage with this spirit and not to give it an audience. Instead of battling, we did the complete opposite. Each time they had a flare of emotions, I had to help them process out of it. I had to help them replace those negative thoughts with future thoughts they couldn't see.

I realized I couldn't be with them all the time to remind them of their worth and purpose, so the Holy Spirit gave me an idea. We found little river rocks that they could hold in their pockets to remind them they were never alone and that God loves them. The rock signified that God had a specific plan and purpose for their lives. It may have not been a cure, but it served as a practical way to reach out to them when I wasn't around.

I later began to speak to the rocks and started to prophesy over them as if they were my children. I know it may have seemed weird, but I felt I needed to do this. I was being guided by the Holy Spirit. My small jewelry business, Leila's Corner, began from this. I started to make small stone necklaces and earrings that others could benefit from as well.

God knew what we were going through and wanted us to utilize our struggles not only for ourselves but for others. We felt this was why God was leading us to travel and sing over the places we went. Our first and primary job was to blanket the spirit of suicide with love wherever we were led to go because we felt suicidal candidates were future intercessors being killed off at a young age.

To start, we believed we were called to sing over the land and prophesy life over the state of Washington, Ireland, and our home of Hawaii. We were open to whatever God had called us to do and be ready and flexible when necessary. We bought our homemade jewelry to the places we visited to encourage those who needed it, and in return, they could keep it or give it to a complete stranger. We used it as a starting point to introduce our loving God to whomever God wanted to bless that day.

So loving our kids through the process has been the hardest thing we have ever had to face together as a family. I wanted an instant fix, and I learned that I had selfish intentions. God was dealing with me to just be a mom and love my kids through their struggles. My children had to establish new habits, new traits, and a new way of thinking. These were my Barn Owls, and I was training them in love and modeling faith.

Prophetic Numbers

"Teach us to number our days that we may gain a heart of wisdom" (Psalm 90:12). On this entire journey of *Shema: Assemble the Barn Owls*, God has magnified and given us clues and several specific numbers that kept popping up in our lives, travels, and, most importantly, our faith journeys.

Even more amazing was how we discovered this. Over time, we had a sense of peace even in our trials. When those numbers popped up, we knew that God was with us, which gave us confirmation and helped us stay in peace.

This gave us confidence in the hardest times we faced. Although some Christians would call this bible numerology, the Holy Spirit was leading the way. God created everything, and the devil tries to distort it and make it his own. However, God teaches us and gives us knowledge in these areas. Everything—including numbers—was made for us! Many people do fear studying numbers because of a lack of understanding. God is all about numbers, Genesis is filed with numbers, I am simply showing you how God spoke to us.

I do not practice reading numbers from an unknown book or read the stars or crystals or any other mythical element. I hide myself in God's heart and use the Bible for my best understanding of everything God made for us. The enemy has a field day, making it his domain of idol worship. If we know that God made these things available for us, why do we allow the devil to misuse them? Why do we allow the enemy to pervert beauty, humanity, and creation's elements? Nature was made for us to glorify God and help draw us closer to Him. Untouched subject but we must seek it out. Let's participate in his world, our world.

The Holy Spirit has highlighted the numbers nine and six for about the last three years, maybe longer. At first, I didn't take it seriously, but the Holy Spirit was clearly trying to talk to me and trying to show me that he is in control of every detail of our lives. Later, I explain how Joseph discovered those specific numbers so that you can see how God communicates with us.

Numbers have played a huge role in opening up a refreshing and exciting communication level with God. This has personally been a secret code within our family. Numbers have given us confirmation so that we know we are on the right track. For example, these Scriptures—Proverbs 25:2; Romans 8:22; Hebrews 11:1; and Psalm 105:6—are Joseph's and my favorite passages in our faith journey:

- Proverbs 25:2: *When you add the numbers 2 + 5 + 2, they equal 9.*
- The next three Scriptures, added together, also equal 9:
  - Romans 8:22: The numbers 8 + 2 + 2 equal 12. 1 + 2 equals 3.
  - Hebrews 11:1: The total of 1 + 1 + 1 also is 3.
  - Psalm 105:6: The numbers 1 + 5 + 6 equal 12, and then 1 + 2 equals 3.
- The final answer is 3 + 3 + 3, which equals 9.
- When you add 9 from the first Scripture with 9 from the next three Scriptures, the total is 18. Again, 1 + 8 equals 9.

Now I didn't go and find these to make them add up to nine. Joseph and I started to recognize this pattern one day in our journal. We were especially blown away that the final total of all the numbers together from all the Scriptures still equaled the number nine! We received confirmation after confirmation! Only God could do that. The number nine showed us it was time for our marching orders; we began to look for it everywhere and played an exciting game with the Lord.

Later, we discovered God was trying to talk to us about childbirth, which is a nine-month process. The number nine also represents a harvest, the fruit of the Spirit, the spiritual gifts, and fullness of development. Romans 8:22–24 says that the Earth moans and groans in childbirth.

Joseph and I constantly have things magnified to us in many situations. I am sure this happens all the time with everyone, but are we looking? Are we listening? Are we in Shema? If we are, we become more aware of what God is saying.

We have seen the number nine on our license plates, rental cars, and hotel room numbers. We have even seen it show up on our plane tickets and seats, including special dates on our calendars. In addition, scriptures, receipts, past events, milestones from our past, and both my birthdate and Joseph's birthdate also equal the number nine. Strategic clusters of number are added together until it totals a single digit. We keep searching mysteries out, and again and again, we won't stop until we learn what the Holy Spirit wants us to discover. It became so much fun, but later this awareness saved my husband's life.

The second number that was highlighted to us was the number six. We first see the number six in Genesis 2:7 (and those numbers also equal nine), but on the sixth day, the Lord created man and breathed life into man's nostrils.

Many people relate the number six as the number of man or the number of the beast. That may be so, but in actuality, God breathes an ongoing breath into man. This was not only on the day he was created, but God is constantly breathing continual life into him every day, every hour, every minute. Joseph and I experienced this huge revelation firsthand in our faith journey, but later, it was put to the test.

If it weren't for this revelation, I am not sure I would have made it through the toughest trial that was about to hit my home. Shema in its pure form catapulted us into God's destiny. I also knew if plan A didn't work, God always had a Plan B to get us back on track. It may take longer, but God will have his way if we allow him to guide us through it all. You will be in a position to encounter the supernatural. When you allow your mind to be open and expect God to speak to you.

As we pressed on to what God was calling us to do, I looked to see if our kids would assemble behind us and fall into place with the same or a better walk with the Lord. We knew God was calling us to a new strategy and depth, but I worried about our legacy, our children; I wondered if our six owls would follow suit behind us.

Calculate the Numbers

As a man who paid attention to details, Joseph was led to calculate each section of the entire Ireland trip by miles; the outcome was fascinating. God is so specific and masterful with numbers. When you are done with this book, you will begin to search for your family's numbers as well.

When reading prophetic messages and numbers, be sure your sources are biblical. I can't emphasize this enough. Discernment is key. Many legitimate websites and books will help you gain an understanding of prophetic numerical sequences; however, be careful not to read too much into the meaning of other perspectives. You can question and go with your gut instinct because if you are being led by Ruach HaKodesh, he will show you. I sometimes read dream interpretations from Spirit-led prophetic ministers to help open up my mind and receive wisdom and knowledge. But I still double check with God because only he can give understanding. I check to make sure the interpretations are not my own but from Ruach Hakadesh. Your revelation must resonate from God.

This is not a form of Greek mythology called ornithomancy that uses the birds of the air to read or predict their omens and future. The Babylonians, Persians, Assyrians, and Romans practiced all sorts of divination. I am also not talking about Kabbalab, Chaldean, or Pythagorean numerology either, which are all types of divination. This is not what we are about. Also the birds of the air and other animals, including a donkey that God spoke through, were used many times in the Bible to bring forth a revelation or deliver a message. God is a God of secrets and mysteries. Why not find them out?

In Daniel 2:27–29, the prophet praises God and interprets the king's dream:

> Daniel answered before the king and said, "As for the mystery about which the king has inquired, neither wise men, conjurers, magicians nor diviners are able to declare it to the king. However, there is a God in heaven who reveals mysteries, and He has made known to King Nebuchadnezzar what will take place in the latter days. This was your dream and the visions in your mind while on your bed. As for you, O king, while on your bed your thoughts turned to what would take place in the future; and He who reveals mysteries has made known to you what will take place. (NASB)

I can never lean on my own understanding, but by faith, I need to trust the Lord as I move forward; if I am wrong, I keep pressing into learning. There are also so many resources, so I bounce them off my husband or a friend. I sometimes may question an idea because it's not edifying, comforting, or exhorting. It might only bring fear to me or to others, or quite frankly, I can't back it up with the Bible. If so, I tread lightly before adding it to my spiritual vat. I leave room to question the source. If a revelation has a confirmation, I still wait on the Lord to bring me clarification. Some people have told me some strange things over the years, so many times, we just have to trust the Lord first, and He will bring understanding later. First John 4:1–2 reminds us to test the spirits: "Beloved, do not believe every spirit, but test the spirits to see whether they are from God. For many false prophets have gone out into the world. By this you will know the Spirit of God: Every spirit that confesses that Jesus Christ has come in the flesh is from God."

Do not only test others but test yourself as well. You will understand more of the secrets that God revealed to us when adding the numbers from every stop we made in Ireland. The details will blow your mind.

CHAPTER 7

IRELAND: REESTABLISH THE COVENANT AGREEMENT

He remembers his covenant forever, the word that he commanded, for a thousand generations.
—Psalm 105:8 ESV

Preparing for Ireland
September 2018

JOSEPH AND I could not wait; we were like teenagers as we were preparing for our honeymoon trip to Ireland. We were going to meet up with the Holy Spirit. God was putting the details of our trip into motion. God expected us to follow through by faith in obedience since we knew the routine of jumping when he called.

Prices were so outrageous that at times, we doubted. However, the Lord continued to remind us He was in charge and our trust was being exercised.

We registered for our passports since we had never flown outside the US before. We tried to secure a travel date. Due to the expensive roundtrip flights, we took a risk and searched vacations on discount site. We found the best package deal, and the dates fit, so we went with it.

Joseph and I understood that if we were going to make a big decision, we had to wholeheartedly commit. We presented our decision to the Lord and waited on him for instructions. Once he gave us the go-ahead, we came into agreement and, by faith, moved forward. Usually his confirmation came in the final hour. Sometimes I felt he was late, but he was always faithful and right on time.

Our hope is to always believe. In John 11:25–32, Martha's brother Lazarus died and was laid in the tomb for four days. Martha blamed Jesus for being late to help. In response, Jesus raised Lazarus from the dead. Jesus said to Martha, "Do you believe?" She responded yes. Our natural tendency is to strive to make something happen. As Christians we might try to turn our prayers into a passionate religious plea and become a people of works instead a people of faith. Sometimes, like Martha, we just have to believe.

Joseph and I believed together, so no matter what was thrown our way, whether we succeeded or failed, we did not blame the other person. We did all things together; however, this took time to learn as husband and wife. We would pick up where we left off and kept moving forward, knowing the Lord would get the victory. I would like to say that we were always brave Christians. However, we have had our fair share of wrestling with God and wanting things to go our way.

My dad would always say, "Everything is gonna be all right, or "What's good about it, honey girl?" (That's what he called me until my first daughter was born, but I was the first honey girl.) Dad's heart was big, and he always wanted the best for all of us. What father would want it any other way? When he first came to the Lord, he changed his ways drastically and dedicated himself wholeheartedly as a Christian man. He was the patriarch of our family. It was natural and normal to sit and worship at every family gathering; music was always in the air.

One day, I was at home and the phone rang. It was Dad. He could barely talk.

"I can't breathe," he said.

I hung up, put my children in the car, and drove to the house. I walked in, and Dad was in the bathroom, splashing water on his face.

"Dad, what's wrong?" Before he could even open his mouth to answer, he fell right on me, pointing to his head. He was a big guy, and I couldn't move him.

"Dad! Dad! Stay with me, please, Dad!" I was trembling and hyperventilating. I struggled to focus.

"Jesus, help me, please!" I yelled as my younger children watched. I grabbed the phone and dialed 911.

"Daddy, don't leave me, please! Stay with me!" I pleaded.

"Where are you?" The 911 dispatcher questioned me. I couldn't answer. She asked my address, but I couldn't remember. She asked me my name, I told her but frantically answered.

"Don't leave me now, Dad, I need you!" I cried out to the Holy Spirit.

"Charla, stop! Calm down and let me help you!" the dispatcher yelled.

The ambulance arrived, and they rushed my father to the hospital. He had suffered an aorta tear of his heart valve. The doctors performed emergency heart surgery, and he thankfully survived. But he couldn't really talk. We thought everything was fine, but thirty days later, his organs could not bear the stress of the recovery. So he passed, August 9, 2008. I really miss that man.

The night before he died, I didn't want to go to the hospital because my mom told us it looked like he wasn't going to make it. The doctors said we needed to say our goodbyes. I was furious. I didn't want to hear it. We were giving up! We were Christians, for God's sake! I questioned myself. When did we ever throw in the towel? In fact, I felt if I went to the hospital, I would be saying my goodbyes, and I wasn't agreeing with that. I told my mom I didn't want to go because if Dad didn't see me, he might fight to stay alive until he could see us all. However, that wasn't the case. God wanted me to go. So I got dressed and made my way to the hospital.

That day my entire family with my kids gathered in Dad's hospital room. They took him off life support, and he was breathing on his own for some time. His organs were failing, and they gave him medicine to ease the pain. We decided to worship and sing songs about God's goodness as he laid there.

At 7:11 p.m. (even this number adds up to the number nine), he took his last breath. In the quiet, the sunset over Las Vegas gently radiated inside his room. We had never before felt such humbleness and greatness of God's power. You could hear a pin drop in the room; we knew the Holy Spirit was there to collect my dad. We witnessed heaven extended to him. Despite our sadness, at the same time, we were amazed at how much our souls were at peace.

I kissed my dad, but watching my mom say goodbye was the hardest of all. He was the love of her life, and they were inseparable. My heart was beyond broken that day; it was crushed. We sat there in the room, mourning, but feeling God's presence. Dad's soul was gone, he was with God.

I loved the Lord, but as the days passed, I became very upset with him. I was mad, and I wanted him to know it. I struggled, thinking, *I have committed my entire life to you. I dedicated my family and life and all service in every ministry that came our way, and, you just took my dad.* My heart and mind wrestled with God. Healing took time, but the Holy Spirit told me to be completely honest with God. That was my ticket to peace and to carry on in loving him.

I understood my place and that I was his creation and he was my Maker. My perspective started to change, and I knew he loved me even more because I was human and told him how much I hated him. I would cry in such anger, but the same time, I was weeping because I loved God so much. I couldn't understand it. I was totally dependent on him, no matter the outcome. The Holy Spirit helped me through it all, and one day I heard God say, "Everything is gonna be all right." That was my dad's saying. We can plan, but God has the final say. This lesson was a huge turning point for me concerning faith.

Ireland: Reestablish the Covenant Agreement

No matter what, the Bible says all our days are numbered. No matter what we face in this life, win or lose, God is still with us. With my dad, life didn't turn out the way I wanted, but God gave me courage that day to push the envelope and take risks, risks that only included him. Trust him in the journey. That day, I realized I needed to keep his legacy alive through music. No matter what, I needed to keep my dad's covenant agreement with God concerning worship alive through our bloodline, and this trip to Ireland was our opportunity to do just that.

God had this upcoming Ireland trip in store for us if we would give him the benefit of the doubt as he took us on this journey. Win or lose, we were doing it together with him, so it was all worth it. We would jump and know that wherever we landed, we were in God's hands. Of course, I thought we were crazy for listening to God telling us what to do and when and how to do it. Yes, but we needed to just trust him. We felt everything was gonna be all right.

Once we found a great travel deal, we prayed and purchased our tickets right away. We normally don't have a stash of cash lying around, but we paid under three thousand dollars, which included car rental, accommodations, meals, and roundtrip flights from Seattle to Dublin. We would stay at four different castles on our ten-day honeymoon with the Lord. We knew it was God! It was our calling, birthed of our new ministry to worship over the land. As we moved toward the goal, God gave us strategic revelation on what we needed to do on the trip.

My mom, who is thankfully a passionate intercessor, called a gathering of prayer warriors to start praying for us. These ladies were a backbone of our faith adventure. They came to our house; spent time with us in prayer; gave prophetic confirmation and words of knowledge; and blessed us. One particular word came from my mom. She said we would be welcomed and we would know that God was directing us by showing us specific signs. One sign would be a rainbow, promising he would never leave us on this trip and that the rainbow would let us know he was leading us.

That night I had a dream. Joseph and I were standing at the edge of a high cliff, facing the Atlantic Ocean in Ireland. The wind was blowing so hard that my hair was blowing away from my face. We worshipped, not with our voices but with Joseph's stringed guitar. The Lord's voice, hovering over the ocean waters, echoed over this country. "Thy kingdom come, thy will be done in Ireland as it is in heaven."

After I woke from the dream, I wondered why we were facing the ocean and not the land. I thought that if we were singing over the land, we should face the land. When I questioned the Lord, he answered my question in Genesis 1:2.

The Spirit of God hovering over the waters in some translations of Genesis 1:2 comes from the Hebrew phrase *ruach elohim*, which has been interpreted as "a great wind." *Rûach* (רוּחַ) has several meanings—"wind, spirit, breath"—and *elohim* can mean "great" as well as "God."[8]

I interpreted the dream to mean that our worship was drawn into heaven, hovered with God over the ocean, and dispensed onto the land with strong winds, ruach elohim. Our sound of worship was connecting us to the wind and water. The Lord said, "We will seal the atmosphere with spiritual resin, a prophetic worship vibrating across the plains. We will set a standard in this new era." I didn't understand all the details, but this is where we had to start, offering our worship to be one with God and letting ruach elohim bring a newness of life on Ireland.

After that dream, I asked, "Why Ireland? Why barn owls? Why was God connecting us to them and to Ray Hughes?" I felt there must be more.

Proverbs 2:10 says, "It is the glory of God to conceal a matter, but it is the glory of man to search it out." So in addition to singing over the land, we needed to understand more. I looked for further confirmation, and boy, did we get it.

I felt led to research barn owls of Ireland since I had studied barn owls of Washington state. I had no idea that the owls were once numerous in Ireland but were now an endangered species. The predators hunted for rodents and rats that were dying in the fields due to pesticides. Unfortunately, the second-hand poisons killed them as well. In the past, farmer settlers depended on the owls to protect their crops from destruction instead of

Ireland: Reestablish the Covenant Agreement

using pesticides. How prophetic. However, the chemical methods led to the decline of the barn owl population. Later, wildlife legislation protected Ireland's barn owls and took active measures to find safe places for them to repopulate.

Two months before we were headed to Ireland, the BBC reported a remarkable event in Lough Neagh. After I read it, I understood the spiritual meaning as well.

> The biggest brood of barn owls in Northern Ireland has been recorded near Crumlin, County Antrim. The world welcomed five chicks of the endangered species on private farmland near Lough Neagh. The nest site, located in an abandoned outbuilding, normally produces one to two chicks per year. Ulster Wildlife volunteer Ciaran Walsh said conservationists from across the UK and Ireland were "in total disbelief" at the new arrivals. There are an estimated 30 to 50 breeding pairs in Northern Ireland, with only three known active nest sites.
>
> "When they started to breed, it was a bonus, but then I realized five chicks had appeared, and I was amazed," said Mr. Walsh.
>
> "I kept counting them and then I let out a squeal — it was pure excitement. I cracked out a cider and shared the video of the five chicks with the other volunteers. Nobody could believe it — we were blown away."[9]

The miraculous return of the barn owl chicks was an amazing sign; God was clearly communicating, or maybe we were listening more closely.

As we were planning our trip, Joseph and I were dealing with a buyer from Hawaii who was trying to buy a parcel of land Joseph's ancestors had passed down to him. We had no idea he had land, so we needed to research Joseph's bloodline. This had nothing to do with Ireland—or so we thought.

Thank God, Joseph's younger brother did much of the legwork of their family tree, making it easier for us to trace. We found out Joseph's bloodline traced back to the house of King Kamehameha of Hawaii. His ancestry runs deep in the Hawaiian kingdom; he is a descendent of the *kahuna nui,* or the high priest Hewahewa, who served in the court of King Kamehameha. God blew our minds, and we had to connect the dots in this life puzzle. I can't impress on you enough to never stop seeking God in everything. Be relentless in finding the treasures he has for you. Search things out, and you will find them! This is how God works. Our revelation was mind-blowing.

Hewahewa was one of the ruler's top aides in healing medicines and brought wisdom from their gods. He operated with a prophetic gift. When King Kamehameha died, his son Kamehameha II tasked Hewahewa in 1819 with abolishing the Kapu system and burning the religious temples and idols dedicated to worshiping false gods.

In 1920, Hewahewa converted to Christianity and led the Hawaiian people by influencing worship of the God of Abraham, Isaac, and Jacob. He brought prayer and hula into the courts to worship Jesus Christ. The Hawaiian king was also a major influence; Hewahewa would be considered a Levitical priest. Joseph's bloodline connected us to an ancestral covenant made centuries ago.

We understood at this point we needed to realign ourselves in agreement with what took place in the past to bring it forth to the future. We had been told many years ago we emanated priestly qualities in our faith. As pastors, we strongly desired to help, encourage, and bring healing to those around us by pointing them to Christ. Who would have thought God was bringing to present a two-hundred-year-old mandated covenant and reestablishing it through us. It might look different from how it was done in the past, but it would be now done with more wisdom and understanding while celebrating Christ within the culture.

Could it be that we would have the opportunity to right the wrongs committed by our early settlers as they spread Christianity? I think so. Their message was right, but the delivery may have been wrong. We are to celebrate all that we are as the Lord made us; in past centuries, Christians did not know how to do that. We realized we needed to bring healing and establish the love of Christ instead of religious politics.

The discovery of my husband's priestly, royal ancestry sealed our call to go to Ireland and minister over the land in worship. Visiting Hawaii was also part of our plans. This was an anointed call—God's vision discovered by us for others.

We learned more about the abolishment of the *heiaus* (temples of worship), particularly one place called Kukuihaele on the Big Island. This heiau, one of the last places to be abolished, became a sacred monument cared for by the Hawaiian people with great pride. However, in 1958, rats and rodents were destroying indigenous plants and sugar cane crops Hawaii requested emergency assistance from the mainland to help stop the destruction. The solution? Fifteen birds were imported from California by the State Department of Agriculture at released at Kukuihaele on the Big Island.

Can you guess what kind of birds were released? *Fifteen barn owls!* Was it a coincidence? I couldn't take it! Was God saying something? I think so. Now Kukuihaele was known on the Big Island as "the land of many heiau." These owls were sent to a place called Kukuihaele, meaning "temples." These fifteen owls could safely clean the land and rid the farms of these rodents and pests. I believe God has chosen spiritual owls to spiritually clean the land.

When you add the numbers one and five, they equal six. The prophetic number six means the six days God breathed life into man. I believe spiritually, God sent in these physical owls as a sign of a spiritual cleansing over the land. Now it's our turn to gather other anointed owls to clean the land.

Ireland, the Emerald Isle

When we landed at John F. Kennedy International Airport, we waited for twelve hours before checking in at Aer Lingus terminal because the check-in counter wasn't open yet. We had to wait outside, where there was only one coffee stand and limited seats. Joseph and I waited to grab a spot in the corner. We tied our bags to us, secured our luggage behind our chairs, and took turns sleeping. We found the bathrooms and a place to eat a snack. We sat and talked about people passing by and browsed social media on our phones while trying to keep a positive attitude. The Holy Spirit was teaching us to wait. This was the kind of wait that both the mother and father experience during a pregnancy as they expect the birth of the child.

Again, the Scriptures proved true. Romans 8:22 talks about this waiting and expectation.

When a woman is expecting, the wait seems forever. As a mother of six, I know about this. We may try to hurry along the process with home remedies. However, the baby will come when the baby is ready. God loves it when we embrace the wait and learn what he wants to do through that process.

Finally, Joseph and I boarded the plane headed for Dublin, a smooth flight until we entered Ireland's airspace. The pilot announced we were encountering strong turbulence as he prepared to land. We landed early on a windy morning. We sensed we had completed the first mile marker. I teared up as if I were returning to a land that I was connected to. I couldn't explain the feeling as if I were home, though I had never been to Ireland.

We went to pick up our rental car. Normally I drive, but Joe said he was driving this time, I was okay with it because the steering wheel was on the opposite side. We got into the car and just drove. But we soon ended up getting caught in the wrong lane, and Joseph couldn't turn off. Cars behind us were speeding by, and the area was not safe, so we had no choice but to just keep driving. We were lost.

At first, we tried to show patience with each other, but that didn't last long. We were driving down rough streets you only see on TV. We worried that someone would attack us. I began to yell at Joe, and he began to yell at me. Our iPhones had no service. Our honeymoon trip with God began to turn into a nightmare of yelling at each other as cars were honking their horns at us. The pressure was on.

We found a gas station; we took some time to regroup. We still had no data. Luckily, Joe knew how to read old-school paper maps. We finally set up the GPS from the rental car agency, which we should have done before we even left the airport. We drove around in circles a couple of times. We were tired and spent. I began to cry, and we agreed that we didn't come this far to argue but to meet up with God. We started out again but still drove to the same gas station five more times. We stopped to collect ourselves again and again. We were not going to give up. We asked each other for forgiveness and set our sights on the first destination: Dunboyne Castle Hotel.

Ireland: Reestablish the Covenant Agreement

Dublin to Dunboyne Castle, Twenty-Four Miles

As we drove around, the wind was picking up. We were island people, and we treated it as Hawaiian trade winds so didn't think much about it. We were focused on our GPS; we didn't even turn on the radio. Finally, we found our way to the castle and went toward the check-in counter.

When we got our hotel, I noticed our room number was 329. The numbers $3 + 2 + 9 = 14$. The numbers $1 + 4 = 5$, which added up to the prophetic meaning of grace. Why grace? Grace is God's unmerited favor. God was protecting us through what was about to happen to us over the next couple of days. Divine grace is his goodness toward those who have no claim on it or reason to expect it. See, we didn't know we had arrived in a severe windstorm that was worsening by the hour.

We went to the room, showered, and napped. When we woke up, the wind had picked up tremendously. Even so, that night in Dunboyne Castle, we slept so peacefully. Ray Hughes called to check up on us and made sure that we were safe. A local newspaper reported on the storm, that we were in on our trip there.

> Storm Ali hit the country on September 19th, bringing force 11 winds, with gusts on the west coast reaching 142km/h (79 knots), the highest level recorded since the Mace Head station in Co Galway opened in 2004.
>
> Two people were killed and tens of thousands left without power after Storm Ali swept the country in mid-September. Elvira Ferraii from Switzerland died after the caravan she was staying in was blown onto a beach in Co Galway and electrician Matthew Campbell from Belfast died in the Slieve Gullion Forest Park after he was hit by a falling tree while working for the Northern Ireland Water Utility.[10]

We didn't have time to meet Ray or minister over the castle grounds. The next day, we had to go to our next destination. We wondered what was happening. However, God told us that atmospheres shifted in the region by our presence and our agreement with Him. We believed we were the calm in the middle of the storm, the five-card draw of grace occupying the area. Why? Because of our faith and the position of our hearts. We believed this! Our presence made a difference.

Scripture models this for us. In Acts 5:14–15, the apostle Peter, who walked with Jesus, carried faith: "Yet more and more believers were brought to the Lord—large numbers of both men and women. As a result, people brought the sick into the streets and laid them on cots and mats, so that at least Peter's shadow might fall on some of them." (BSB) Similarly, in Acts 19:11–12, the apostle Paul carried the power of the Holy Spirit and performed miracles: "God did extraordinary miracles through the hands of Paul, so that even handkerchiefs and aprons that had touched him were taken to the sick, and the diseases and evil spirits left them." (BSB)

We should search for signs and wonders all around us. Signs will be magnified and confirmed in your spirit. Perhaps *you* are the sign. Ray Hughes advised us to pay attention to the elements that were all around us when we arrived in Ireland. The numbers helped us confirm the direction and the season that we were in. With the Holy Spirit's wisdom, we could understand revelations that were illuminated to us. We can decipher the Holy Spirit talking to us through numbers. Isaiah 55:5 gives us a glimpse of the wisdom we can possess and even the impact on nations: "Surely you will summon nations you know not, and nations you do not know will come running to you, because of the Lord your God, the Holy One of Israel, for he has endowed you with splendor."

The next morning, we walked the grounds of the Dunboyne Estate, confident of God's presence with us. We blessed the area and declared that all who came to the castle would be drawn to the Lord by way of divine appointments and that God would call more people to this area to fulfill his plans and purposes.

As we were getting ready to depart, the wind was picking up. Before leaving, we captured a towering rainbow in front of us. My mother had prayed that we would see God's approval through rainbows that greeted us during our entire trip. God was sending these signs to lead us. We took time to stop and take it all in.

Ireland: Reestablish the Covenant Agreement

Dunboyne Castle to Rock of Cashel, 111 Miles

We set up the GPS, turned on the radio, and headed toward the Rock of Cashel. It was a way off, but we felt that we needed to go there. The roads were narrow, and the locals were crazy, fast drivers. We were sure they knew we were from the US because we drove slowly and cautiously. We passed through small towns that looked like those you see in movies about Ireland.

The winds grew more intense on our drive there. The locals scurried about, almost in a panic, when we stopped for gas. We pushed on and finally reached the Rock of Cashel. Joseph and I didn't follow the tourists on the walk up to the castle; we made our way toward a hole in a fence and walked on the outskirts of the ruin.

As we looked over the surrounding land with the breathtaking view, I began to weep as the wind blew my hair back. I began to sing, "Sing alleluia to the Lord" over and over again. The wind rustled all around me as I imagined a blanket of love was covering the land as the wind carried my anointing to wherever God wanted it to go.

Joseph asked, "What's wrong?" I didn't know how to answer him. I just felt as if my tears were covering the land. Joseph hugged me and said, "I wonder why God sent us here first?" We didn't know. We were just following him by faith and doing what he asked us to do. Later, he revealed why, but by faith, we had to follow.

On our way into the ruin, another rainbow appeared. At the ticket counter, we were advised that the storm was picking up and they were closing. They told us that a woman had died due to the severe windstorm. Her car was blown off a cliff. Joseph and I realized the seriousness of the situation. God was protecting us since we had to get back in our car and drive to our next destination.

After returning from our trip, we researched the Rock of Cashel. We knew the importance of this site, but we later understood why we were led here first. This ancient royal site of the kings of Munster first attained importance as a fortress. Its origins as a center of power dated back to the fourth and fifth centuries. Two of the most famous people of Irish legend and history are associated with the Rock of Cashel. St. Patrick was said to have arrived in Cashel in AD 432 and baptized King Aengus, Ireland's first Christian ruler.[11] The second was Brian Boru, crowned high king in AD 990.[12] He was the only king able to unite all of Ireland for any significant period of time.

We felt we were present to reestablish a mandated covenant agreement. A covenant order was established between parties from the past that needed to be resurrected and reconfirmed in the present, essentially continuing the work Christ began. St. Patrick had passed long ago, but we could pick up where he had left off to carry the cross and the message of God. We could bring Christ's love to the world. This was not a religion but a relationship. We could be used by God to restore covenants, just by our presence on the land.

Rock of Cashel to Kilronan Castle, 149 Miles

We had to backtrack to get on the right road toward Kilronan Castle. God clearly had us on a strategic path. Our presence in the land was making a difference and extending our faith level. God strategically mapped out our drive. We still don't know the full impact of what we did. However, God will reveal it to us later.

Through the years, Joseph and I have been pioneers. We love to go to new places, experience new things, and make things happen. Instead of being blindsided by risk, we have learned to embrace risk and the process. God meets us all the time. He is faithful although sometimes not in the ideal way we would want. Even so, he is present. Let your faith be authentic and real. When this happens, we grow and are challenged to believe in the impossible.

As we drove north to Kilronan Castle, the wind became so strong that we could feel the pressure on our car. Trees were falling on the road, and home trash cans were flying. We thought about pulling over, but we felt God telling us not to stop We needed to reach our destination before nightfall. Reports on the radio advised us of widespread outages due to trees falling on wires and homes.

We pressed forward while our GPS directed us down a back road. As we drove deeper down this tight road, we seemed to be driving to a secluded hunted house. I was really scared and started to silently pray, *Lord, please help us get there.*

I told Joe to turn around, but he said that God told him not to stop, so we pressed forward.

Finally, we came to an opening and turned the corner to the entrance of the beautiful Kilronan Castle. As we passed through the gates to a road that hugged the cliff side overlooking a lake, I felt as if I had entered a scene from *Beauty and the Beast.* The sun began to pierce through the clouds.

I've seen beautiful places before as I traveled with my parents all over the US. However, the beauty of this place took by breath away. I felt like a princess, and Joseph was my prince, taking me to his castle. Silly, huh? As a girl born and raised in Hawaii, I felt giddy. I was experiencing this beautiful land together with my husband. We were in awe.

We turned the corner, and this exquisite castle surrounded by acres upon acres land stood before us. As we got out of the car, the wind continued to blow swiftly. We walked up to the entrance and checked in. Our room was located on the east wing facing this beautiful lake. Our room number was 116. This was the number 8 (1 + 1 + 6 = 8), the prophetic sign of new beginnings.

The elegance and captivating view greeted me as I opened the door to Room 116. I wondered, *How we could have gotten this room? How could we have been so lucky?* God knew it was our time to receive his best. I felt he was rewarding us for being obedient and listening to him. God was there, and his favor was manifest upon us. This room had the best view.

A palpable peace surrounded the estate grounds—in the air, in the trees, and on the lake. I leaned my head out the window with no screen as the wind rustled through the trees. I could not leave the window. The wind started to die down. Joe and I sat down on the bed and thanked the Lord for getting us to our destination safely. This was so much more than we could ever imagine; it was our time with him. He knew our hearts; we didn't have to pray or say anything. We were in his presence and He in ours.

That night, we enjoyed a meal fit for royalty. We always considered ourselves as royalty as God's kids, but we were experiencing it for the first time on a different level. We called the kids back home in Washington to tell them of our great travels. Honestly, we also called to make sure the house was still standing. We shared our excitement about what God was doing. After the night's activities, we laid in bed, we could only think about worship over the land in the morning. We woke the next morning to sunlight streaming into our room on our bed. With coffee in hand, we sat in bed, looking out our open window. Silenced embraced us while God spoke to our souls.

We started down the trail toward the lakeside with our instruments and camera. Joseph led the way while playing his ukulele, which echoed through the trees as if we had a microphone. Our purpose was to just sing and allow our faith to vibrate across the land. Our sound waves would penetrate the surrounding atmosphere. We prophetically sang songs of life and of God's love through our worship. One of the songs we sang was "Way Maker" by Leeland. We sang it over and over at the water's edge. Incredibly, the trees swayed to our singing; the wind was responding as we sang. It was incredible to witness this again.

In the distance, people approached, so we stopped. A couple of sightseers from Switzerland walked up and said, "We could hear your singing from up here, and it sounded like angels."

Joe and I laughed. They asked where we were from and we told them Hawaii but that we now lived in Seattle. They asked if we could walk with them. We didn't think anything of it, so together, we walked around the outskirts of the lake and returned to the Castle. They asked if they could buy us coffee. We utilized this time to explain what God told us to do on the land. I don't know if they really understood it, but before they left us, I blessed them with a special piece of handmade jewelry from Leila's Corner. In return, they pulled out a map and told us of key places we needed to visit. We welcomed their advice. After our meeting, we went back outside under a big tree on the property and began to sing again.

We didn't care who heard us. The clouds began to part as the sun pierced through the clouds and shined on us. It was so serene and kind of mysterious. We again felt his presence. I was reminded of that peaceful feeling in that hospital room when my dad passed away. It almost felt like that. I will never forget that feeling as if God extended heaven to us that day.

After we worshiped, we were ready to have some fun with the Lord; we went down to the spa room where there was a beautiful pool. We imagined this was how royalty took a bath. In fact, they called it the king's bath. Pillars were throughout this underground spa with four columns around the pool, reflecting dark blue water. The lights were dim, and we had the place to ourselves. So romantic! Joseph and I didn't know how to act; we felt out of our league, but God had arranged our honeymoon with him. After our second night festivities included a beautiful dinner and a tour of the castle. Then we were off to bed.

Why we were led to minister at Kilronan's Castle? On the opposite side of the road from Kilronan Abbey is the Holy Well, associated with St. Ronan's daughter, St. Lasair. The well is surrounded by a low wall with a plaque commemorating the visit of Pope John Paul II in 1979.[13] Later, we met a woman who told us that the Holy Well was the site of prayer meetings where they worshiped and called on God to heal the land. God had us again reestablish covenant agreement with those we had no known relationship with. Again, our presence was needed shifting atmospheres to bring in the new anointing.

Kilronan Castle to Mullaghmore, Thirty-Nine Miles

The next day, we left Kilronan and traveled north to Lough Eske Castle, but we had a few stops to visit based on the recommendation of the couple from Switzerland. Our route took us along the coastline of the Atlantic Ocean, and we passed through beautiful countryside towns, ruins, and scenic beachside pastures. It was like a scene from the PBS drama *Poldark*.

We drove past Sligo and took a side road to the oceanfront. We were greeted by a rainbow again. We stopped to take it in. The Lord was leaving signs to confirm we were on the right track. God seemed to be greeting us around every corner. The wind was still blowing, and ocean waves crashed against high cliffs below. We stopped and peek over the edge of the cliff at the ocean. The ocean mist sprinkled on my face and reminded me of home—Hawaii. The only difference was the cold air and the Atlantic Ocean. God was our tour guide.

That couple from Switzerland told us to go to Sligo and visit Mullaghmore. It was God's divine plan for us to be there. We learned about Father Michael O'Flanagan, a Roman Catholic priest, a popular social Irish republican. He was also the vice president of the Irish Agricultural Organisation Society, a proponent of land redistribution. In 1914, he was transferred to the parish of Cliffoney in north Sligo.[14] He was known as the rebel priest because he fought for the people's right of cutting turf from their inherited land. Father O'Flanagan rallied the people after mass one day and led his congregation to get enough land for each family so they would not freeze in winter. He came against government agencies who were trying to allocate bog land and turf rights to the more prominent society members. Because of his passion to fight for the people, his political beliefs, and the views he held, he was suspended from the priesthood. I find it ironic that when God's love arises, the religious spirit attacks.

He also traveled to America to find investors for an agriculture and industry campaign for the people. Three miles from Cliffoney parish, he found a more suitable location in Mullaghmore. Each night, before going to bed, Father O'Flanagan went down to the pier for a swim. In his journal, he wrote: "When one goes out swimming at night, at least in Mullaghmore at that time of the year, every stroke starts thousands of little phosphorescent lights shining in the water, with the result that one feels surrounded by a halo like the picture of a saint."[15]

Not only was he a passionate priest for the people's rights concerning land, but he was also an inventor—the inventor of goggles. His advertisements stated: "Father O Flanagan's patent bathing goggles surround your eyes with airtight chambers and enable you to see like a fish through the water."[16]

Did you connect the pieces of this puzzle yet? The land and water were part of my dream. The goggles represented godly vision and his love for the land and its people. Again, we were there to *reestablish a covenant agreement* that Father O' Flanagan started in the physical. God now had a spiritual covenant for the people of that land. God allows us to seek things out and find hidden secrets to glorify him.

We drove toward Donegal. Further north, we found an abbey and stopped to view the towering ancient headstones of men and women of the faith. As we returned to the car, we encountered another rainbow.

Donegal to Lough Eske Castle, Five Miles

We left the abbey for Lough Eske Castle and entered through the back gate. We were greeted like royalty again although we aren't prominent people. It was almost uncomfortable this time. The staff served us so well. We walked through the castle and took in the beautiful modern décor.

We stayed in the carriage house. We rested, dressed, and went to the main dining hall. As they seated us at our table, we felt like movie stars. We stayed one night, and the food and wine were magnificent. I was addressed as "ma'am" and Joe as "sir." The next morning, we were the only couple in the breakfast hall. *What's going on God?* I thought. The place was all ours. God is so good like that.

We made our way through the north of Ireland. We imagined that our presence was a spiritual fragrance of God's love. As we drove, we proclaimed God's love for the people and the places we traveled. We understood God had us there to align ourselves with other believers in the spirit who had already been standing in prayer for these matters for years. As we were finishing up our tour, we understood why we were there.

We proclaimed that we would do the following in every place where we traveled.

- Worship or sing over the land, changing the atmosphere from death to life, helping people awaken to their destinies
- Invite people to yearn for Ruach HaKodesh through our intimacy with God as we shared his love with others
- Join with other believers that have long stood on sacred grounds to bring revival
- Follow the clues, signs, and wonders that uncovered his plan to be manifested in that land

We were encouraged and strengthened by Scripture that promises that these kinds of signs would follow us in Christ's name. John 14:12–14 says:

"Very truly I tell you, whoever believes in me will do the works I have been doing, and they will do even greater things than these, because I am going to the Father. And I will do whatever you ask in my name, so that the Father may be glorified in the Son. You may ask me for anything in my name, and I will do it."

Our travels continued with more signs and revelations and even more rainbows. Our final days were horseback riding as we traveled the Wicklow Mountains. We visited the movie locations for *P.S. I Love You, Braveheart,* and the TV series, *The Vikings.* We continued to minister on. We met beautiful people and learned history that we connected with. These stops reflected on how God spoke to us and how we responded to (Shema) him. Please, pay attention to what you can as not everything will be magnified to you. But you will sense and know what is happening in the Spirit.

As we finished our time in Ireland, we visited with Ray Hughes and his wife Denise. Our special conversations confirmed many things about the land and its elements as God was leading us as spiritual barn owls.

Before I go any further, I want to mention how much I loved Ireland. Joseph and I had no prior in-depth knowledge of the places we traveled to. We knew of the destinations where he led us and to be obedient and by faith, we sang worship over the land we traveled to. When we returned home, the Lord told me to search out the places we went since we were there to *reestablish a covenant agreement* and agree with what had been started there. I was so blessed to find out why we went to these specific spots. This is how God wants us to trust him; we must first trust, and later, he will bring us understanding. But we must obey and trust.

Continue on and you will find the detailed calculations of our trip to Ireland and how the Holy Spirit led us in a personal understanding of these numbers. Keep in mind all the different ways God speaks to us and allows us to hear him. In this season, we were hearing him through numbers.

When we returned, Joseph reviewed our trip since he is such a detail-oriented person. He was led to search the different distances we traveled on our journey. The results were astonishing! Just for fun, I decided to add his numbers that joseph detailed of our trip to see what the

Ireland: Reestablish the Covenant Agreement

prophetic numbers totaled. This was so detailed that only God could have orchestrated it.

Let me explain these calculations. All together, we had fourteen legs on this trip with three or two stops in each leg. At the end of each leg, we calculate the total miles traveled. Our first Leg below of these three destinations when added together totaled our prophetic number seven. Let me try to break it down for you.

From our home to SeaTac Airport, the total miles were 40. From SeaTac to JFK Airport, the total miles were 2,414. From JFK to Dublin Airport, it was 3,187 miles. When I added up all those miles, it totaled 5,641. (40 miles + 2,414 miles + 3,187 miles = 5,641 miles.)

This total amount of 5,641 miles can all be added together to *create a single digit (5 + 6 + 4 + 1 = 16)*. Although sixteen is a prophetic number, God wanted us to bring our numbers down to a single digit to communicate with us. So again, *we separated the 16 (1 + 6 = 7),* and here you see our revealed digit is seven. In the prophetic, the number seven means "complete." More in-depth detail is available on the meanings of the numbers at various websites online. Always bring your added numbers to a single digit. The highlighted numbers below show all the miles that we covered on that leg of our trip:

Our home to SeaTac Airport	40 miles
SeaTac to JFK Airport	2,414 miles
JFK to Dublin Airport	3,187 miles
Total = 5641	
(5 + 6 + 4 + 1 = 16) *now the* **16 (1 + 6 = 7)**	
Prophetic number = 7	

Dublin to Dunboyne Castle	24 miles
Dunboyne Castle to Rock of Cashel	111 miles
Rock of Cashel to Kilronan Castle	49 miles
Total = 184	
(1+8+4=13 now 13 (1+3=4)	
Prophetic number = 4	

Kilronan Castle to Mullaghmore 39 miles
Mullaghmore to Donegal 28 miles
Donegal to Lough Eske Castle 5 miles
Total = 72
(7+2=9)
Prophetic number = 9

Lough Eske Castle to Clonmacnoise 128 miles
Clonmacnoise to Fitzpatrick Castle 93 miles
Fitzpatrick Castle to Iveagh Garden Hotel 10 miles
Total = 231
(2+3+1=6)
Prophetic number = 6

Iveagh Garden Hotel to Fitzpatrick Castle 10 miles
Fitzpatrick to Molly Malone Statue 10 miles
Molly Malone Statue to Powerscourt Estate 15 miles
Total = 35
(3+5=8)
Prophetic number = 8

Powerscourt Estate to Killegar Stables 3.5 miles
Killegar Stables to Poppies 3.5 miles
Poppies to Powerscourt Falls 8 miles
Total = 15
(1+5=6)
Prophetic number = 6

Powerscourt Waterfalls to Guinness Lake 7 miles
Guinness Lake to Glendalough 11 miles
Glendalough to Molly Malone Station 31 miles
Total = 49
(4+9=13) now 13 (1+3=4)
Prophetic number = 4

Molly Malone Statue to Fitzpatrick Castle 10 miles
Fitzpatrick Castle to Dublin 27 miles
Dublin to JFK Airport 3,187 miles
Total = 3224 = 11
Prophetic number = 2

JFK Airport to EWR 33 miles
EWR to Ramada Plaza 5 miles
Total = 38 (3+8=11)
Prophetic number = 2

Ramada Plaza to EWR 5 miles
EWR to Penn Station NYC 17.5 miles
Total = 22.5
Prophetic number = 9

Penn Station to EWR 17.5 miles
EWR to Ramada Plaza 5 miles
Total = 22.5
Prophetic number = 9

Ramada to EWR 5 miles
EWR to JFK Airport 33 miles =11 miles
Total = 38
Prophetic number = 2

JFK Airport to Crown Plaza 2 miles Crown Plaza to JFK
Airport 2 miles
Total = 4
Prophetic number = 4

JFK Airport to SeaTac, 2414miles SeaTac to Home 40 miles
Total = 2454
Prophetic number = 6

When Joseph added up the calculations of these prophetic numbers from all the legs of our Ireland trip, it came to **67 = 4. (6 + 7 = 13; then 1 + 3 = 4.)** The number four prophetically has different meanings from different perspectives. The website for Pour It Out Ministries (www.pouritout.org) is a great resource. The number four has a personal meaning for me, especially when we went through Joseph's surgery. (I share this story in the upcoming chapters.) The number four was on all his hospital rooms.

Jodi Hughes of Pour It Out Ministries shares these prophetic insights about the number four. The number four represents an open door, creative miracles, creative opportunities, and an open invitation to encounter God. He calls us to come up higher, obtain a fresh perspective, and increase our vision. The number four represents a breakthrough season of victory. Revelation 4:1 speaks of John the apostle's prophetic dream with an invitation from God to come up higher: "Then as I looked, I saw a door standing open in heaven, and the same voice I had heard before spoke to me like a trumpet blast. The voice said, 'Come up here, and I will show you what must happen after this'" (NLT). Psalm 44:4 praises the God of victory and breakthrough: "You are my King and my God, who decrees victories for Jacob." The number four also speaks of creation, the Earth, or creative works. Jodi Hughes observes that on the fourth day, God had finished with the material creation.

In Hebrew, the fourth letter is *dalet* and is represented pictorially as an open door, likened to an open tent door found in the tent of meeting.[17] The open door implies an invitation to enter God's presence. When seeing the number four, take note of what you are doing at the time as it may be an open-door season. Be open to a fresh perspective as you come up higher. Watch for an increase of the seer gifting to see with greater clarity. God was declaring and decreeing victory for me and for you. Let me encourage you to align with what God is saying as you enter the open door. Here I showed you how the Holy Spirit communicated to us with numbers. You can not put God in a box. Explore and follow his lead and he will give you revelation.

CHAPTER 8

POSITION OF THE HEART: OUR BATTLE HAS ALREADY BEEN WON

Many are the plans in a person's heart, but it is the Lord's purpose that prevails.
—Proverbs 19:21

THROUGH OUR YOUNGER years, our approach to intercessory prayer seemed to be expressed in a battle mode, especially regarding our trials. In my culture, people normally love and fight hard. This characteristic invaded our prayer life. As spiritual warriors, our prayer took on a fight pattern of passionate prayer. While that was positive, we had to be skilled in prayer as well, skilled in understanding when to aggressively decree the gospel and silently maneuver the fight.

If we are not careful, the enemy can trick us so that we pray in circles when the battle has already been won by Jesus. Prayer has no right or wrong ways to do it because God is patient in how we offer up our prayers. He wants us to engage in prayer but more so to connect in a relationship with him. However, there is a right way and wrong way to engage spiritual warfare. There is prayer for the sick and for your family and for the world, but to pray defensively against the demonic, you need God's wisdom and timing. We learned this the hard way. If you don't know what I'm talking about, just ask the Holy Spirit to guide you and he will. I challenge you to gain understanding in this, just be wise and be cautious.

Jesus said, "The Son can do nothing by himself; he can do only what he sees his Father doing, because whatever the Father does the Son also does" (John 5:19). Many times, the backlash from aggressive prayer can worsen the problem. Through trial and error, we realized that at times, the best thing is to speak life over a situation and take up a stance and position of the heart. This means to understand who you are in Christ and to stand in confidence in it. It's an understanding of our faith level.

Over time this understanding protected us from a direct manifestation from dark entities that would attack us through sickness, imbalanced emotions, or financial hardship and much more. I have witnessed intercessors attacked and drained and even suffer within their immediate family or worst on themselves. The only way to be successful in your prayer life is by understanding who you are in God's kingdom and where you stand in it. This is called third-heaven intercession. We need to know how to operate with this mindset as this will change perspectives on how to engage. Third-heaven living is essential in my life. Understanding this and being humble allows us to stay safe in God's covering when we pray. I confidently know that I can access his authority but, at the same time, revere him as my Creator. The fear of the Lord is our strength. our heart needs to embrace this mindset, which I learned when we got the devastating news about Joseph.

Lemons: Putting Shema to the Test
July 4, 2019

Have you ever heard the saying, "When life gives you lemons, make lemonade?" Any other day, I might have gone with it, but the day I'm going to tell you about wasn't like any other day. It was going to cost more than just lemonade. I wasn't going to accept the tart, bright-yellow fruit thrown at us. I thought my metamorphosis was over, but God was not done yet with us.

On that horrific day, my spirit went into defensive mode and rejected what was on the menu. I was not going to entertain it, and I needed faith for something else. I felt I was mature enough in my walk with the Lord to draw from my heavenly account and trade my lemons for miracles. When putting this book together, I thought I had it all planned out, but God suddenly interrupted my plan and his plan prevailed.

For a month, Joseph had not been acting like himself. He was strangely distant, almost fading in and out of being the man that I loved. I thought maybe he was dealing with a personal matter, and I just couldn't pinpoint the problem. We had a well-balanced routine after being married for more than twenty-eight years. I usually knew what made him happy, angry, and even what he was thinking. Yes, we could even finish each other's sentences and prayers. However, what transpired next gave me a clear indication we were in trouble.

"Let's pray," I said. Joe wasn't feeling well.

"Bleep prayer!" he yelled.

I was totally surprised, shocked, taken aback, and hurt. What had just happened? When we were first together, he sometimes cursed like a sailor. This happened once in a while at work or when he got really angry, but this? To say *the 'F" word*? It hit my heart; this wasn't just toward me but toward our God.

I wondered, *Who is this man sleeping in my bed? You may look like my husband, but you are not him.* I was so worried. What was I up against?

A couple of days went by, and he seemed to be drifting further and further away from me. He would go to work and come home and stare into nothing, not saying a thing. It was deep, as if he were looking in the abyss. His eyes were almost empty. Where was my husband? He would go to work, and I would sit in silence and cry my heart out, pleading with God to help me understand.

One day, he went to work without even saying goodbye. I woke up early, thinking he must have been late because he left without a goodbye kiss. I slowly began my day and pleaded with the Lord, "What should I do? Help me, Holy Spirit. There is something wrong." He had not been sleeping in my bed for almost a week. We had a couch in our room, and he sometimes sat there, falling asleep. But that day, he had slept on the couch. I was desperate, so I decided to sit on the couch to pull myself together and pray for Joseph, hoping to get some kind of insight as to what was going on.

As an intercessor, I was pretty in tune with the Holy Spirit. I laid in Joseph's spot for a very long time, praying, and I cried myself to sleep. I regularly homed in on objects around me to get some kind of feeling or insight as to what was happening. The Lord would reveal things to me and direct me in prayer like that at times. It took me a long time to understand this. When I was younger, I just shrugged it off. However, I was born with this sensitivity and could not just will it at any time. The Holy Spirit allowed me these senses at his discretion. I wasn't in control of this ability at all but was totally dependent on his lead.

As I reflect, I could sleep in a room and dream of all the things that happened in that room. Other times, I could walk in a room, and the Holy Spirit would point me toward an object he disapproved of, like a piece of jewelry or a movie about witchcraft even a piece of clothing, that was cursed. This insight over time revealed we had to physically remove items from our property. Or sometimes we just prayed over it. As I grew in my faith, I sensed things on strangers. Even as I hugged them I knew what to pray. While raising my kids, I could sleep on their pillows and see where their minds were. Again, I wasn't in control of this but just grew in my gifts from the Holy Spirit. God willed it, only when he wanted.

Unfortunately, this time when I woke from the couch where Joseph had been sleeping, I sensed nothing. Worry and fear were setting in. More days passed, and Joe was so quiet and barely eating, I tried to start a conversation about work, He only responded with sighs, as if it were hard to talk. He began to skip snacking, which was his all-time favorite pastime. I mentioned to the kids that "something was wrong with Daddy."

They responded, "Maybe it's just work, Mom,"

I felt there was more to it than work. I feared he was having symptoms of dementia or the start of Alzheimer's. I didn't want to think that way, but it entered my mind. I, like many others today, started to search the internet for signs and symptoms for further insight as to what was going on. My last attempt was spending time in the car doing our weekend errands. We always had great conversations and enjoyed our car ride together. I figured I could question Joe, but again, he barely responded. I ask him detailed questions to see if his memory was intact. He answered but with few details. I questioned Joseph about our past on traumatic incidents we both failed in miserably. These types of incidents He could recall, which scared us. I tried to remind him how God had brought us through triumph and victories as well. I was sure he would remember these key episodes, but they didn't jar his memory. I was losing my best friend and felt so empty.

That morning July 4, my world turned upside-down. Joe seemed to be more himself when he woke early. He hugged me and kissed my forehead. We laughed a little and cuddled on the bed, and I started questioning him. As we lay there, I asked him my name, and he told me who I was. I asked him to name all his children. He began to tell me in order: Austin, David, Abigail, Joshua, Elizabeth, and Iokepa. I relaxed, thinking I was worrying for nothing. Within minutes, he began to fade away again.

"Tell me about Abby." I asked Joe about each of our children by name. He didn't respond. I asked him about Abby again, our oldest daughter.

"I like Abby," Joe responded flatly.

I like Abby? Like? He never responded that way about Abby! He always said he loved Abby. I went through each child's name and asked him question after question. He remembered their birthdays but didn't recall detailed information. I was fully depending on the Holy Spirit at this point; my heart was pounding in fear. I was almost on autopilot. My husband's short-term memory was almost gone. *Is this really happening*? I asked God.

"I have a burning feeling here." Joseph touched his eyes and forehead in the middle of my questioning.

"What does it feel like?"

"It just burns behind my eyes." I was already preparing to take him to the hospital.

I continued to ask about Joshie who is now 18 years old which we almost lost him; born a preemie at only four pounds. This pregnancy was a miracle, a turning point in our faith level, experiencing God's grace and favor on us.

The night he was born, I bled so much I barely could walk to the car. I had to hold a towel between my legs to keep Joshie from falling out. Joseph declared in the car while my dad drove us to the hospital, "We will not lose this baby. God gave him to us, and we will not lose this baby."

Later, we talked about how we both envisioned ourselves reaching up toward heaven, touching the cloak of Jesus, just like the woman with the issue of blood in Luke 8:43. This woman bled for twelve years, desperate for a healing from Jesus. She came up behind him and touched the edge of his garment. Immediately, her bleeding stopped. Jesus knew someone touched him because he felt the power leave him. Jesus turned to comfort the woman and said her faith had healed her. She drew a miracle out of him.

Like Joshie's birth, we believed that our faith, combined with the physical action of reaching toward heaven in the car, would grab Jesus's attention and that the Apanas drew power out of him for this miracle.

Joshie's premature birth was a big moment in our lives. When I again attempted to ask him about this, to jar his memory, Joseph could not talk about it. My questioning continued, but it only made him confused and angry. He zoned out again.

As I continued questioning him, I held back my panic. I gathered our kids to come to my room and question their Dad. Thank God, I could do that. My two oldest boys had just moved back home, so all our children were present. One by one, they came into the room as I explained what was going on. Worried, they hugged their dad, seeing he was not himself. We quickly prayed and decided that I should take him to the emergency room.

I collected my bag, phone charger, and a pair of socks. These were no ordinary socks; they were our cabin socks. I grabbed the socks to see if Joe would remember them. These socks were so special to us.

In 2017, on my birthday Joseph took me on a weekend cabin getaway, away from the kids and the busyness of life. The theme was the roaring 20s, and when I walked through the doors, I was amazed, surprised, and even blushing. The gift was unexpected but surprisingly welcomed. Who knew this would touch my heart so deeply? Joseph knew me better than I knew myself. I would have never envisioned wanting something like that, but my heart received Joseph's tender thoughtfulness.

As if we went back in time, we entered a magical setting: a small cabin with a small kitchen and an old stove. Beautiful 1920s china was properly arranged on the table with a small birthday cake with my name on it as the vintage radio box played music from the 1930s.

As the music played, Joseph grabbed me, and we started to dance. All I could do was cry as Joseph began to pray and thank the Holy Spirit for being there with us. I had fallen more in love with him over the years since the very first time we had met. But this was beyond that kind of love; this was a three-union kind of love: me, Joseph, and the Holy Spirit. I held on to him tightly as we danced. God knew my heart and how I melted for a man that loved his presence like I did.

The night grew cold. I had forgotten to pack my socks; however, Joseph brought an unopened package of thick insulated work socks (our special cabin socks). Two pairs were in the package, one for me and one for him.

We both agreed that I would never wash my pair of socks because this time was so special for us, a rekindling with the Holy Spirit. We would later joke about it all the time, our own inside joke. We joked that we had permission to walk around the cabin in only our birthday suits and socks. God reminded me to gird my feet in peace and walk in his peace as I did in that cabin, with those socks.

Now, God knew these socks would remind me of that time and of what he had spoken as we went to the emergency room. I placed them in my bag so when I got to the hospital, I could try again to jar some of Joe's memory.

While driving to the hospital I asked the Holy Spirit to lead me to what hospital we needed to go to. I thought, *Lord, if you intended to get my attention, you've got it. I am all yours and now lead me.* I drove right up to emergency at Swedish Edmonds. Joseph insisted on walking up to the entrance doors. He was dragging his leg and holding his arm toward his chest at this point.

I struggled to maintain my composure as I dashed to the front desk of the emergency room. "My husband is having a stroke!" I directed him to sit down nearby.

The admissions staff quickly alerted the nurses. They came out with a wheelchair and took Joseph through the closed doors. Within a matter of minutes, the nurses weighed him and tried to get as much information from me as possible. Once in a room, they checked his vitals. Other staff then whisked him away for a CAT scan and X-rays. Everything was happening so fast, but I tried to keep calm. After a series of tests, Joseph was brought back, and all I could do while he was lying in bed was to rub his face and kiss him.

"Everything is going to be okay, honey. We will find what is going on. Look what I have." I pulled out our cabin socks from my bag. "Remember these? Our cabin socks?" I hoped Joe would recognize them, but he did not. Even when I tried to tell him, he didn't seem to notice.

I wanted to cry and have him hold me in his arms and tell me everything would be all right, but he couldn't. My best friend wasn't there. I felt so alone. I hoped that when he saw the cabin socks, he would agree with me that we would be okay. I then began to tell him the story, and slowly he began to smile and laughed as he remembered our time together at the cabin. I recorded that moment on my iPhone to show him later.

The doctor came in as I sat next to Joseph on the bed.

"Well, we got back the report and viewed it. We are sorry to tell you he has a lemon-sized tumor in his head. I am so sorry, Mrs. Apana. I am so sorry," the doctor repeated.

Joseph did not seem scared but just laid there quietly in the bed while fear engulfed my body. I shook uncontrollably. Joseph just looked at me wordlessly.

The Doctor continued. "We need to rush him over to the Cherry Hill campus, and they will have to do emergency surgery. He is losing his memory because his brain is swollen. They will have to operate and see if they can remove part of the tumor."

The doctor came around and held on to me because Joseph could not. He was in another place and did not even cry. On the other hand, I was devastated, and unraveled before the doctor. I was so scared to call the kids and tell them what the doctor found, but I had to.

My eldest son Austin answered the phone, and I told him to put me on speaker. My voice cracked as I began to tell them what was wrong. However, Austin said, "Mom, don't panic. He's alive, not dead. He is alive. He's still with us. Let's focus on what needs to be done now." My eldest son's strength was rising, and he continued to declare, "I'm *not* losing my dad today."

I handed the phone to Joseph. He responded to Austin and talked normally with him without skipping a beat. To my relief, he clearly remembered Austin. Austin said, "Dad, we'll get through this. God's got this! I got the kids, and we are going to pray now!"

Despite everything Austin had been through over the many years, struggles concerning suicide and depression, when push came to shove, my firstborn was front and center in hearing God's voice and standing firm. He stood up and took his place as the eldest son and rallied the family together to stand in faith and to contend for our peace. He led the charge as we positioned our hearts to focus on peace. He began to counsel me. "Be in peace, Mom. Stay in your peace so you can hear what God wants us to do." My barn owls, my watchmen, were starting to assemble.

The staff prepped Joseph to be taken by ambulance to the neurosurgical unit in Seattle to prepare for the operation. I was in full disbelief, stunned, holding onto Austin's lead. I felt like a deer, standing in the middle of the road looking straight into the headlights of an oncoming car. The ambulance came, and even the EMT said, "I'm sorry," in sensitivity to this news. It still felt as if it were the end of Joseph's life. I heard that phrase repeatedly, but I had to contend for our peace.

I listened to what I needed to hear: the Holy Spirit's voice. I couldn't hear him physically, but I keyed in to his voice in my spirit. I began to see magnified numbers, signs, and phrases from other nurses and doctors to confirm he was still with me. I was gaining my peace as I gained understanding.

These signs were all around: the hour of the clock, Joseph's patient ID badge, room numbers, floor level, and even the license plate number on the ambulance that transported us. I also recognized specific words that the staff and doctors were using, words that only God uses with me in prayer and through my life. I felt safe, knowing God was with me and I was not alone, despite the enemy's lies. If I were focusing on the enemy, it would have destroyed me, so I chose not to. These life-giving confirmations gave me the peace I needed. This made me more sensitive to find the next secret as I moved forward in this trial.

I rode in the ambulance as the medics drove us toward Swedish Cherry Hill in Seattle. Once there, they rushed Joe to his room in the intensive care unit. The staff prepared him to receive medication to reduce the swelling in his brain. The lemon-sized tumor was aggressively pushing on his brain so that he was bleeding internally.

Soon the medication began to work, and his swelling was dissipating, finally bringing back some normalcy from Joseph. He began to talk and realized what was happening. We didn't dare entertain thoughts of his death. We didn't dare go there. During the brief time I had with him, we had to be in agreement as to what would happen next. We both agreed that God was handing out miracles and we were in line for one.

As all of this was happening, I continued to pay close attention to what was around me, waiting and expecting the Holy Spirit to reveal his next secret messages. I was watching the clock, room numbers, and everything around me as God was magnifying what I needed to see, hear, and understand. I am not going to lie; I was definitely terrified.

"Mom, hold on to your peace." Austin's voice repeated in my mind. Again, as different doctors entered the room they said, "We are sorry." This made it harder for me to hold on to my faith. Again, I had to contend for our peace.

Nurses and other staff dropped in, wanting his blood work done or checking his vitals. His vital signs added up to the number nine. This was our number. I was almost in unbelief because who else other than God could do just that. Even as I write this, it still seems as if it were all a dream.

I waited to talk to the surgeon assigned to Joseph's case. He finally came in to visit with us. I tried to stay extremely positive. With a small seed of hope from the medical staff, I felt maybe, just maybe, I would receive a favorable second opinion. That was not the case.

The surgeon introduced himself to us. He explained what they were going to do and how severe Joe's case was. He asked if my family was there for support and if he needed to wait to talk to the entire family. I suggested we FaceTime or call them. "Whatever is easiest," he said. I made the call to our children.

Austin answered. I told him the doctor was with us and he wanted to address him as the eldest. Austin placed the call on speaker phone so the rest of his siblings could hear.

"I wanted to let you all know what is going to happen to your dad," the doctor started. "We found a large mass the size of a lemon in your father's frontal left brain. There is no other option at this point but an emergency surgery to take it out. We are not sure what we will find until we go in, but our *hope* is to go in and take as much of it out as we can, but what I need from you is *your approval* and the entire family's *agreement* for us to do this job the best as we can." (Here, I am emphasizing the words that the Lord highlighted to me in my spirit.)

As the spokesperson for our family, Austin responded quickly. "Doc, I know God sent you to us, so do what you need to do, and I trust you will take it *all* out," Once again, we followed Austin's lead as he reminded us to stay in agreement, the agreement of *positioning our hearts and minds* in the direction of faith. This was not an aggressive prayer or some battle minded thinking. We felt strongly that we should not fight this disease or even raise up our spiritual swords to attack the enemy. I might add this attitude was strongly recommended in my earlier years as an intense intercessor. That was far from our minds, but our hope was to stay in God's *peace*. However, we knew that clearly the devil was trying to destroy our family, by taking my husband.

This surgeon and God's timing aligned with us in this situation. God used this doctor to set the atmosphere for all of us coming into godly *agreement*.

I did not know what religion Joe's surgeon was, but I knew God could use anyone to get the job done under his terms. The Scripture that I often refer to is: "It is God's privilege to conceal things and the *king's privilege* to discover them" (Proverbs 25:2, emphasis added NLT).

The revelation from this Scripture told us that this doctor was considered a king. His wisdom and experience placed him in a specific field of work as a king in the field of neurology. This king went to medical school and was very experienced in taking us down a road that he searched out, like the Scripture says. Long before we crossed paths, he labored in this field to prepare to reap the benefits or privilege of his kingship. We hoped that

Joe would victoriously come out of the surgery which the doctor seemed to prophesy, and the Holy Spirit allowed me to witness it.

I recognized how God was using a complete stranger, this surgeon, to set the pace in bringing godly agreement and spiritual alignment before the surgery began in that room where I would not be present. Nevertheless, although I did not expect it, God's presence was with this surgeon talking to us.

God was speaking, and I needed to be listening more than praying. This was in the Shema, meaning we cried out to God, and He was replying. This was not in warfare; it was leaning our attention directly to God as he responded to us. He was speaking through this doctor. Though I was shaken and still experiencing much fear, God was trying to get my attention right in the middle of my storm even as my physical body was unraveling. I kept myself together until after the doctor left. I needed some air, so I left the room and went down the hall toward the elevators. I called my mom. Even though God was still connecting with me, I was still scared.

Mom was not in Seattle; she was visiting my younger brother Chad and his wife in Redding, California. My mom would schedule periodic visits there to see her youngest grandson. I was looking for some kind of reassurance from them and from her.

When I heard Mom's voice on the phone, I just fell to pieces, like a little girl who needed her mommy. Panic started to set in again even after God had just reassured me that things would be okay. My younger brother Chad got on the phone to calm me down and said the same thing my eldest son Austin said: not to be shaken by fear.

Chad continued, "Char, we pray coming from a place of victory, not going toward it. Let's come in agreement that Joe will be okay." Confirmation again! My brother said the same thing the doctor said in the room. The word was agreement and was being drilled into my mind. The Lord continued to redirect me back on the path of peace and faith. My emotions were scattered all over the place, and it was a roller coaster trying to get back on track. In every traumatic situation, Joe has always been there with me, facing it together. However, at that moment, my kids and my mom were not physically there. My oldest brother and my kids were on their way to the hospital. I felt so alone, but the strangest thing is that I wasn't.

Position of the Heart: Our Battle Has Already Been Won

After I hung up with Mom and Chad, I turned around and there, standing in front of the elevators, was the surgeon who had just spoken with me and my children in Joe's room. He walked toward me and placed his hand on my shoulder. "*It's gonna be okay.* Everything is *gonna be all right.*" The surgeon confirmed it again, reminding me that God was with me. My brother Chad had just said, "It's gonna be okay."

My eyes were bloodshot at this point from all the crying as the surgeon's words resonated within me. This wasn't just confirmation; it was my dad's famous saying also. "Everything is going to be all right. It's gonna be okay," Dad would say. It was our family mantra. My dad, who had passed almost ten years earlier, was always there to encourage us, and now in heaven, God was allowing his voice to ring over this matter as well.

I collectively added this as another sign from the Lord that he was with me. I needed to stay in *peace* to be able to hear his voice. Quite frankly, in my condition, my own prayers would have been out of control and full of emotion rather than faith. Even in emotional chaos, God can still intervene. This was a different level for me though, so I knew the Holy Spirit wanted me to be quiet and recognize his constant presence. He continued to remind me he was there and not to worry.

Many intercessors say that the devil cannot understand your heavenly language. True, because I used to have this mindset as well. However, later through much time with the Holy Spirit, I understand that the devil is not so dumb. He can definitely understand the emotion coming from you as you pray in the Spirit, leaving you lacking confidence and vulnerability in understanding your position as a child of God. Your responses to situations will reveal the victory of the battle or the defeat before you even open your mouth. This revelation made sense.

The Holy Spirit wanted me to remain quiet, listen (Shema), and be navigated by my confidence in really knowing him and knowing what the Scriptures say about who I am in him. He wanted to lead me in this detailed process. If I were pleading my case in warfare prayer, I would have not been able to hear or *Shema* him.

Normally, when I am in deep intercession, I am pacing back and forth, expressing my heavenly language as a war cry. But that would have been a distraction in this specific situation. This situation was not actually a battle. If I engaged in battle, it was a sign to the enemy that I had already lost because I forgot who I was in Christ. Mind you, as an intercessory prayer warrior, it was extremely hard to shut my mouth. I had to be in maturity and not fight every battle the enemy says is a battle. God's Son had already won this battle when he died on the cross. In fact, it was a distraction! However, I was maturing and learning a new way of maneuvering in faith and peace, which was Shema.

The Holy Spirit wanted me to partner with him to learn how to steer this ship of prayer and intercession as he led me to experience the journey in hearing, seeing, and watching a miracle unfold, not only for me but for others to witness firsthand. I could not take my eyes off the one who could bring forth the blessing from heaven, and I needed to set up a spiritual atmosphere in my mind so that I could receive the miracle God was about to deliver to me and my family instead of being distracted by the enemy.

Now don't get me wrong, there is a time and place to cry out to God and seek his protection to unload many of the world's burdens that intercessors carry. But you must know who you are and with faith that does not panic and or aggressively fight a battle that has already been won. As an intercessor in this situation, my first prayer response toward the Lord was to cry out to him and only him. I had to trust him to hide me in his care and release my emotions and fears and place my godly fear in him. I cried and repeated these words in my head, *Have mercy, oh, Lord.* This humility placed me in the upper room of God's presence, showing the enemy I was not in control but God was. The enemy was not up against me, but up against my Daddy God in heaven. I was preparing to release the work of the Ruach Hakodesh.

I humbled myself before the Lord, and He redirected my prayer like this: *If anyone is going to take Joseph from this Earth, it will be you, Lord, and no one else.* The Holy Spirit then said to me, *Charla, be in confidence that I am in control and just listen—Shema me.*

I waited to hear from Him. I soaked in worship songs and saturated myself in worship music, expecting a miracle. I was contending to get my heart in the right position, a position of faith and peace. Was I terrified?

Position of the Heart: Our Battle Has Already Been Won

Yes! My focus was to stay calm and at peace to contend for my confidence and to hold a position of my heart to stay in peace.

God already knew what I wanted, what my heart longed for: that I would not be without my husband and that our kids would not be without their father. However, as much as Joseph's life would bless me, God wasn't done utilizing Joseph on this Earth. I did mention to the Lord that when he formed Joseph and me as a couple, we were *one person on Earth. So how could he separate that? How could he separate his unity?* Since God joined us, I redirected my prayer toward him. I said that He was a faithful God and that I believed that our destiny and plan was not finished. We needed to be together to accomplish that plan. God made me and knew how much I loved Joseph and how I was feeling.

As the surgical staff prepared Joseph for surgery, our kids finally arrived at the hospital. At this point, Joe was acting like himself again due to the temporary medicines to help bring down the swelling. He was talking and laughing, and the kids were taking pictures in the hospital room. All six of my children seemed to have taken on this level of confidence as we surrounded him.

Austin told me that prior to coming to the hospital, the kids had time to sit, pray, and cry almost uncontrollably. It was incredibly sad to witness, he said.

As the eldest, he had strayed from the Lord the most because of our earlier years in ministry, which left many unhealed wounds and trauma. Though at times he fell short (as we all do), he loved the Lord no matter where he was in his struggles. This situation was marking him as a leader to his younger siblings in trusting in the Lord and believing in God's faithfulness in bringing us through this valley.

As a mother, I was so blessed to see my children manifest what I had taught them at a young age. When they blossom and bring hope to us parents, I am thankful of the witness that they do have a personal relation with the Lord and can hold their own faith when we are not around. This was a huge breakthrough for Austin because he had been through so many tough circumstances. He was innately strong with a natural ability to lead, and lead he did with his younger siblings when we could not lead. In fact,

I followed him. My firstborn prayed with his siblings and told them: "We are not losing our dad today. We are gaining a miracle."

We did not have time to talk to one another, but the Holy Spirit had given us this same mindset before the kids came to the hospital. We were all connected in the spirit realm although they were miles away, praying at home. The children all gathered and cried together over their fears of not having a dad; Then they shook it off and positioned themselves in expectation of a miracle. After our kids met with their dad, my kids and I went into the hall where we hugged each other and cried. My youngest son, Iokepa, was trying to make sense of it all. I took a moment to privately reassure him.

Iokepa tightly held on to me. "Mom, I'm scared."

I told him, "Don't be, son. It's our turn."

"Our turn for what?" Iokepa questioned.

"It's our turn because God is giving out miracles today for the Apana family! And we are in line to get one. God is giving us an opportunity to show him off, and we won't let him down. All we need to do is stay in peace and believe!"

Back in the room, the kids loved on both Joseph and me as we came together and prayed, before his surgery. Thanking God for our victory for the expectation of the great things and favor on us as a family.

My oldest brother, Clyde, my biggest supporter, finally arrived at the hospital; he stood in the place of my dad. He walked into the room that night before the surgery and grabbed Joe's feet and stood at the end of the bed, praying. God was doing a deep work and healing in my brother as well. Clyde and my sister-in-law, Lynn, stood in faith for Joe and me. My dad would have done the same. He was taking his place as my dad's barn owl. God was putting together the pieces of this puzzle, making me feel safe in my surroundings.

Pastor Dan from Sonrise church came to pray and anointed Joseph with oil, which was important to me. They also brought a cloth that read, "Ain't no grave gonna hold me down" as a reminder that God is into miracles. The phrase was inspired by an old hymn that Molly Skaggs revived in her rendition of a praise song called "Ain't No Grave." We were gravitating

Position of the Heart: Our Battle Has Already Been Won

toward that song even before all this came about. We had confirmation that we were on the right track and in God's timing.

The doctor came to bring Joseph into surgery. The staff asked if we wanted the cloth on his body while they were operating. We said, "Yes." The doctors told us they would tape it on his skin. This cloth would be seen by the doctors who were performing his brain surgery, reminding them that God was using them to bring about a miracle. How wonderful the Lord is! Whether they believed in my God or not, they witnessed his presence and power. The word to hold us up in prayer went out to everyone we knew. We could feel the support and peace of all those backing and surrounding us in prayer to help us through.

Again, I want to emphasize that we did not do spiritual warfare or call out the devil like we did in our younger years. This was key in coming out of this valley. We needed to focus and be ready to hear the Holy Spirit, Shema. But this was not easy as we were in the middle of a storm.

The hours leading up to Joseph's surgery quickly approached. The staff said the operation would probably take four to six hours. They came to get him, and we all expressed our love and didn't dare say our goodbyes. That was not even a thought as they pushed him down the hallway on his gurney.

I walked with Joe down the hall as far as I could go. I cried and asked the Lord to hide me in his wings. I was confident in the Lord, yes, but my heart was breaking at the same time. I was majorly contending to not be in fear. The staff said I could stay in the waiting room with my entire family. However, I felt I needed to be alone and focus on what God was telling me to do. I needed to let God control my spirit and lead me. Listening goes beyond listening with our ears and consists of observing and trusting with our entire being, doing whatever he tells us to do at that moment.

I felt led to sit in Joseph's hospital room by myself and relax and sleep. I know, right? How could I sleep at a time like this? All I thought about was the story of Jesus sleeping in the boat during the storm. He was in peace while his disciples panicked. At this point, God wanted me to rest and sleep and totally trust in the Lord. I gave myself completely to his will and released all my fears to be carried away. The Holy Spirit was leading me to sleep as Jesus did.

Joe's bed was gone, and only my chair was there in the room. I looked at the clock, took a deep breath, and said, "Okay, Holy Spirit" as I clutched the blanket the nurse gave me earlier. I pulled it up to my neck and closed my eyes.

I stretched out my legs and crossed them, leaning my head back. I began to release myself into God's Spirit. I can't tell you how I did it. I just focused my heart and mind in union with his. In my head, the Holy Spirit said, *Charla, I need you to just follow my lead.* I found myself in perfect rest. It was as if I were in a movie, as if my spirit were almost transported and taken to the surgery room. It felt like that scene from *Scrooge* when the ghost of Christmas Past came to visit him at night and ordered him to rise and follow him. The Spirit touched his heart, and the pair exited through a window and flew, transported back in time.

That was how I felt as my spirit left my room. The Holy Spirit took my hand and led me to the surgery room. I could not tell you what the room looked like; all I could see was the bed where Joseph was lying and two hands working on his head. Not much was clear though, for some reason, I could see a lot of pink tile. The Holy Spirit led me to spiritually talk to Joe. "Honey, I'm here. I'm right here with you. I want you to relax because God is doing something. God's hands are all over this situation. We just have to follow his lead."

My heart pounded, and in a millisecond, a revelation dropped in my spirit. This was Joseph's heartbeat, beating quickly, the Holy Spirit revealed. I then prophesied over Joseph's body and the doctors in the room as the Lord engulfed the room with his presence. Led by the Holy Spirit, I spoke into his future. "Joseph, this is our next level to enter into our new beginning. God said that his plan is to prosper you and give you a hope and a future. If he will prosper you, he will prosper me, because we are one, not separated but one being. God joined us in marriage, a couple united since the day we said yes to each other." I continued to prophesy to him and over the doctors and allowed the atmosphere to come into agreement with me. My vibrations of faith were moving across the room.

As led by the Holy Spirit, I spoke words of our future together. It was the sound of my voice, but I was not speaking. The Holy Spirit was speaking through me. I was encouraging my own spirit as well. I thought I could hear my breathing, but it was God's breathing.

While sitting in Joseph's room, the Lord reminded me of when Joseph and I first began singing worship together. While praying and singing, we became immersed in the Holy Spirit realm. God's presence moved so gently on us so that we forgot about time and sang for hours. God's presence became so heavy in our room; we would weep because, in our hearts, we knew it wasn't us anymore but *Ruach HaKodesh*.

The Holy Spirit sang to us and over us through our own voices. We worshipped and cried together and received a specific anointing meant just for us. This was a covenant from God to us, to be blessed as one person. As we sang together, we looked at each other and knew exactly what God was saying. This unique power with the anointed vibrations of his sound moved through us to come out of us. As we agreed with him, his power flowed through us as we made music with our Maker. His anointing manifested over us and later, as we ministered to others, over our children, and even the land we spiritually occupied.

The Holy Spirit reminded me this could only be achieved when we did it together. When we sang with others, it was nice, but it didn't have the same effect as when Joseph and I sang with his spiritual weapon: Joseph's guitar. His instrument sealed the deal, making it even more powerful. We were dedicated to God's will and this made a big difference.

This was the covenant God blessed us with years ago. God wanted me to renew this covenant and proclaim it as Joseph was in surgery. I was agreeing with God and his plans. He reminded me of his promise that we would reestablish covenant agreements for others that went before us. I was reestablishing covenant agreements for my dad's unfinished calling on Earth. I wept, thinking, *What do I pray, Lord?* "For the Holy Spirit will teach you at that time what you should say" (Luke 12:12). God was doing just that.

I was listening (Shema) and focused on how God was navigating me and my family. Our heavenly account was getting a big withdrawal that day. The Holy Spirit reminded me to remind the Lord that Joseph needed to *live* so that we could fulfill his covenant here on Earth as it is in heaven.

I continued prophesying. "If I am alive, so are you, Joseph." I imagined my words spoken out loud in the operating room as I spiritually stood there. "If I am complete and whole, so are you, Joseph. Be of great joy, honey, God is doing a great thing to show himself off as the great miracle worker that he is. Right here, right now, God will show our kids how powerful he is when we humbly seek his direction and trust him." I celebrated and thanked Jesus for that.

In the Spirit, my voice continued to echo through the surgery room. My heart began to beat more quickly. I knew it wasn't my heart, but I was feeling Joseph's heartbeat. I then saw myself bend toward Joseph. I whispered, "It's okay, honey. God is here, and the doctors have been appointed by God to take that tumor out of your head. Just relax, honey. Don't be anxious. Just breathe, honey. Just breathe in God's breath, the new life he has for you."

My heartbeat regulated again, so I knew I was in God's complete plan. I then saw an apparition of a male figure in the room and it appeared to lie right on top of Joseph's body. The male figure began to breathe into Joseph's nose—not in his mouth, but in his nose.

I looked more closely as this man took a deep breath and blew into Joseph's nostrils. Joseph's chest inflated. It was *Ruach HaKodesh* the Holy Spirit, Jesus himself. I knew that was why I went through the entire preparation of writing this book. The book would be a tool to share our story, and this moment was our game day. The *Ruach Hakodesh* was fresh in my mind since I was studying it.

This was my opportunity to rise to my place of new beginnings with the Lord. My test was listening to him. My questions were: How well did I follow his lead? How well did I position my heart in faith for me and my family? We were obedient to the Lord. We did not focus on the enemy or on fighting cancer or on giving in to fear. We focused on God's presence and his power. I'm not saying this should be your strategy, but I am saying that God has as a specific plan just for you, no matter the trial or obstacle in front of you.

As Jesus breathed into Joseph's nose, air flooded into his chest. The echo of God's air filled the room and calmed my nerves, bringing me peace. I was settled and focused.

I sat in complete silence and just continued to allow the Lord to breathe into me, knowing he was breathing into Joseph. I was being operated on as well. The truth of Genesis 2:7 came alive to me: "At the time God made Earth and Heaven, before any grasses or shrubs had sprouted from the ground—God hadn't yet sent rain on Earth, nor was there anyone around to work the ground (the whole Earth was watered by underground springs)—God formed Man out of dirt from the ground and *blew into his nostrils the breath of life*. The Man came alive—a living soul!" (MSG emphasis added).

I fell into a deep rest when the call finally came. The team finished the surgery and were prepping Joe to be brought back to the room. The doctor's report confirmed they removed the tumor, a large, lemon-sized ball. A calcium deposit had protected Joe's brain. The cancerous tumor was trying to push its way inside his brain, but it did not enter. It was as if someone hurled a lemon into his head and an armor plate of calcium protected him, stopping the tumor from spreading. While preparing for the surgery, the doctors said they would try to remove as much of the tumor as they could. However, the news came back even better: they took out 100 percent of the tumor. They knew a miracle had happened.

When they brought Joseph back to the room, my boys were there. Joseph got up, looked at them, opened his mouth, and said, "Hi." The nurses were shocked! No slurred speech and all his body parts were moving. Hours later, he was hungry. That day, we received our miracle.

Joseph is cancer-free today. We are living for God and committed to telling our story so other people can Shema God. Stop for a moment right now and thank God for the great miracle he did and what he is about to do in your life while you read this book.

CHAPTER 9

ASSEMBLE THE BARN OWLS: A CALL TO SHIFT THE ATMOSPHERE OF REGIONS

Now Moses was tending the flock of Jethro his father-in-law, the priest of Midian, and he led the flock to the far side of the desert and came to Horeb, the mountain of God. There the angel of the Lord appeared to him in flames of fire from within a bush.
Moses saw that though the bush was on fire it did not burn up. So Moses thought, **"I will go over and see this strange sight—why the bush does not burn up."**
When the Lord saw that he had gone over to look, God called to him from within the bush, **"Moses! Moses!"** *And Moses said,* **"Here I am."**
"Do not come any closer," God said. "Take off your sandals, for the place where you are standing is **holy ground.**" *Then he said,* **"I am the God of your father, the God of Abraham, the God of Isaac and the God of Jacob."** *At this, Moses hid his face, because he was afraid to look at God. The Lord said, "I have indeed* **seen the misery of my people**

*in Egypt. I have heard **them crying out** because of their slave drivers, and I am **concerned about their suffering**. So I have **come down to rescue them** from the hand of the Egyptians and **to bring them up** out of that **land into a good and spacious land, a land flowing with milk and honey**—the home of the Canaanites, Hittites, Amorites, Perizzites, Hivites and Jebusites. And now the cry of the Israelites has reached me, and I have seen the way the Egyptians are **oppressing** them. **So now, go. I am sending you** to Pharaoh to bring my people the Israelites out of Egypt."*

*But **Moses said** to God, **"Who am I that I should go** to Pharaoh and bring the Israelites out of Egypt?"*

And God said, "I will be with you.** And this will be the sign to you that it is I who have sent you: **When you have brought the people out of Egypt, you will worship God on this mountain."

Moses said to God, "Suppose I go to the Israelites and say to them, 'The God of your fathers has sent me to you,' and they ask me, 'What is his name?' Then what shall I tell them?"

God said to Moses, "I AM WHO I AM. This is what you are to say to the Israelites: 'I AM has sent me to you.'

*God also said to Moses, "Say to the Israelites, 'The Lord, **the God of your fathers—the God of Abraham, the God of Isaac and the God of Jacob—has sent me to you.'***

This is my name forever, the name you shall call me from generation to generation.

***Go, assemble the** elders of Israel and say to them, 'The Lord, the God of your fathers—the God of Abraham, Isaac and Jacob—appeared to me and said: I have watched over you and have seen what has been done to you in Egypt. And **I have promised to bring you up out of your misery** in Egypt **into the land** of the Canaanites, Hittites, Amorites, Perizzites, Hivites and Jebusites—*

a land flowing with milk and honey.'

—Exodus 3:1–17, emphasis added

Assemble the Barn Owls: A Call to Shift the Atmosphere of Regions

IN THIS ENTIRE chapter of Exodus 3, God is calling others just like us. He is assembling the spiritual barn owls of your regions.

When we arrived home from Ireland, we wanted to share and teach what the Lord had shown us. We felt led to encourage others to find their own prophetic sounds and minister over their homes, their families, and their lands, and the regions they are responsible for. We wanted to make it practical for home and small group settings.

Joseph and I had interactive teachings on the prophetic and worship in our home for many years. We were learning together and personally involved in other people's lives. These teachings can be done with a large congregation, but we have tailored them toward small groups.

Our Process for Group Study

I will lead you in a process, but you will eventually discover your own. God will show you how to tailor it how He wants it done just for you. Aside from our career path, Joseph and I worked with youth from different churches on the West Coast. As worship pastors, we specialized in children's ministries, intercession, and deliverance at several churches. We learned from our failures. We began to break down our biblical teachings and lesson plans at a third-grade level.

We gave children and adults an opportunity to learn the foundations of worship, prayer, and the prophetic. This allowed a fast-growing congregation to have a solid foundation and understanding so that they could minister in a healthy way. These leaders could then be released to help with the load of new believers that were being welcomed every Sunday. Youth and adults were effective when we practiced listening to each other and to the Holy Spirit. We encouraged their spiritual growth in a great time of learning.

God is into relationships and the interaction of people with each other. He wants us to join together as a body with other believers to bring about his manifested love, not by ourselves but by caring and love for one another. Listening is a manifestation of unconditional love.

During class, Joseph and I gave space to sit with kids or adults and just talk. We wanted to get to know them since we wouldn't be there for their entire faith journey. At least we could have a sense of the spiritual atmosphere they were dealing in their region and maybe even within their own lives or homes.

This chapter will include points on how to facilitate a small group. (This might be your family.) I have divided this chapter up into three sections:

- **First Section.** Understanding holiness and the attributes of God or his spiritual gifts. Our walk with the Lord includes prayers. In some cases, instead of warfare prayer, we just need to position our hearts to receive. Do we need to be holy, blameless, or perfect vessels to hear clearly and minister over the land? No. We will touch on that in this section as well.
- **Second Section.** Key points on the knowledge of the prophetic, and how it can be practically used. Ephesians 4 outlines the fivefold ministry of the church (apostles, prophets, evangelists, pastors, and teachers). You may discover your strong points in ministry, then you can strategically understand and discover your role in your faith journey not only for yourself but for others. We will talk about the Seven-Mountain Mandate, somewhat controversial outside of the charismatic or Pentecostal movements. Also, if you know what area you are called to minister (e.g., government, education), it will help you eliminate confusion as to where your ministry lies. Concerning the Seven Mountains there is some controversy in modeling God's love or control in your scope of influence. Whichever mountain God calls you to, we encourage you show God's love and not force your influence but exercise patience.
- **Third Section.** Interactive lessons to share with your small group and how we do it, step by step.

First Section
Holiness and the Attributes of God

Do you know and love Jesus? You would benefit greatly from having a personal relationship with Jesus, because this is key. That inner voice, the Holy Spirit, will lead you in the wisdom, understanding, and knowledge that you will need in your journey. It's never too late to start. If you don't have that relationship with him, all your insights will be coming from other sources. That would open other spiritual doors that you don't understand in the spiritual realm and cause damage instead of a blessing.

Are you ready to be true and honest with yourself? Are you flexible enough to learn from others? Get to know yourself, make time for personal reflection.

Do we need to be holy to operate in what God is calling us to do in our home or our community? The answer is no because it would take us a lifetime to be a perfect Christian. Nevertheless, we never give up trying to be more like Jesus. We come to him as we are, and we try to make ourselves better people in the faith. Even in our shortcomings, we never stop walking out our faith to help ourselves and others.

Do we seek to be holy? Yes, of course we do, but the holiness we seek is not the kind of holiness we understand. We should seek the attributes of God. Not to be God himself, because only God can be holy. If we were holy, why would we need Jesus?

Many in the Christian community think once you are saved your character should reflect holiness. True, but holiness is a work in progress. If you portray holiness, you tend to mask or cover your true shortcomings. This attitude does not allow you to discover your true self.

The godly attributes we seek are in his presence. If we seek pure holiness with no mistakes, no failures, no wrong choices, and no pain, then how will God bring us closer to him? How would we learn? How will we be able to minister to others? Our failures or shortcomings or sins happen to all of us. If we learn from them and rise above them, we receive a special anointing, which is priceless and is evidence of God's undying power—Jesus at work in our lives.

This is why we need our Savior's conviction even after we get saved, because we are not perfect. We will fall and fall hard at times. This is how we learn, and if we are listening and hearing God (Shema), we gain our approval from him and his anointing. We can have a kingdom mindset, but if we deny our sinfulness, we are walking in complete arrogance on our part. We need humility so that we can learn from our mistakes. By doing this, an anointing—tailored for each of us—will resonate through our convictions.

God requires us to have the attributes of the Holy Spirit, his fruit and his gifts, as holiness. We don't need to strive to get God's attributes; we just need to have a personal relationship with him and the Holy Spirit.

Even godly ambition without reverence or humility can be compromised and defiled if the people around you don't help keep you balanced. A false definition of holiness can form a wall between you and others when God wants us to love them. A religious spirit of thinking you are more holy than others and that you don't fall short will result in an expectation of perfection so that you can never make a mistake. Congregations separate themselves from people because they are not operating in faith, but this harms the church. The world not only needs you, but you need them.

The Fruit of the Holy Spirit

"But the fruit of the Spirit is love, joy, peace, forbearance, kindness, goodness, faithfulness, gentleness and self-control. Against such things there is no law." (Galatians 5:22–23).

Gifts of the Holy Spirit

> Brothers and sisters, I want you to know about the gifts of the Holy Spirit. You know that at one time you were unbelievers. You were somehow drawn away to worship statues of gods that couldn't even speak. So I want you to know that no one who is speaking with the help of God's Spirit says, "May Jesus be cursed." And without the help of the Holy Spirit no one can say, "Jesus is Lord."

> There are different kinds of gifts. But they are all given to believers by the same Spirit. There are different ways to serve. But they all come from the same Lord. There are different ways

the Spirit works. But the same God is working in all these ways and in all people.

The Holy Spirit is given to each of us in a special way. That is for the good of all. To some people the Spirit gives a message of *wisdom*. To others the same Spirit gives a message of *knowledge*. To others the same Spirit gives *faith*. To others that one Spirit gives *gifts of healing*. To others he gives the *power to do miracles*. To others he gives *the ability to prophesy*. To others he gives the *ability to tell the spirits apart [discernment]*. To others he gives the *ability to speak in different kinds of languages* they had not known before. And to still others he gives the *ability to explain what was said in those languages*. All the gifts are produced by one and the same Spirit. He gives gifts to each person, just as he decides. (1 Corinthians 12 NIrV, emphasis added)

First Corinthians 12 outlines each of the nine supernatural gifts of the Spirit, but here is a list of spiritual gifts and their basic definitions:
1. The gift of *wisdom* is the ability to make decisions and give guidance according to God's will.
2. The gift of *knowledge* is the ability to have an in-depth understanding of a spiritual issue or situation.
3. The gift of *faith* is the ability to trust God and encourage others to trust him, no matter the circumstances.
4. The gift of *healing* is the miraculous ability to use God's healing power to restore a person who is sick, injured, or suffering.
5. The gift of *miracles* is the ability to perform signs and wonders that give authenticity to God's Word and the gospel message.
6. The gift of *prophecy* is the ability to speak forth a message of God. A prophet is a spokesperson who delivers the Word of God to people by means of direct revelation.
7. The gift of *discerning spirits* is the ability to determine whether or not a message, person, or event is truly from God.

8. The gift of *tongues* is the ability to speak in a foreign language that you do not know in order to communicate with someone who speaks that language.
9. The gift of *interpreting tongues* is the ability to translate the tongues spoken and communicate it back to others in your own language.[18]

Can You Be Teachable and Shema?

"Then Jesus said, 'Whoever has ears to hear, let them hear.' When he was alone, the Twelve and the others around Him asked Him about the parables. He told them, 'The secret of the kingdom of God has been given to you. But to those on the outside everything is said in parables.'" (Mark 4:9–11).

One evening, Joseph and I were watching the news as they reported on an accident. The person nearly died, and the exact wording the reporter used was that they "escaped" death. We heard the same word "escape" again concerning another story with a different reporter. I am sure it wasn't a coincidence. This is how God gets our attention. Are we listening? Shema.

The guy who helped save the woman in the first story was an EMT/ later we found out he was a youth pastor. If you have ears to hear, you will hear. We heard this message while watching the news that day. Joseph and I felt we should come in agreement with what God were revealing to us through the news, which was this: God will give the youth of this land favor to escape death in a split second because of his covering and his mercy. They will do things they don't even know they are doing because God is in control of their every move so that they can escape a situation and can even save their life from death. In this way, Joseph and I practice listening to what God could be saying in our surroundings.

If you are an intercessor, lean more into speaking life and calling things into existence. Make it *a position of the heart*. Why be at war when God has already won the battles? It's almost arrogant—and certainly lacks wisdom—to war in an area that has already been won. I know it may be hard, especially if you have been praying for a long time, but try not to be a repetitive prayer warrior. You will find more power in *the position of your heart*. Be confident in what God has already done for you. Loving people is a huge component too. It's hardest to love those whom you would have a hard time loving. This is one of God's commandments. God is into relationship and loving all his children. Ask yourself this question: Can you love?

> If I give everything I own to the poor and even go to the stake to be burned as a martyr, but I don't love, I've gotten nowhere. So, no matter what I say, what I believe, and what I do, I'm bankrupt without love. Love never gives up. Love cares more for others than for self. Love doesn't want what it doesn't have. Love doesn't strut, Doesn't have a swelled head, Doesn't force itself on others, Isn't always "me first," Doesn't fly off the handle, Doesn't keep score of the sins of others, Doesn't revel when others grovel, Takes pleasure in the flowering of truth, Puts up with anything, Trusts God always, Always looks for the best, Never looks back, But keeps going to the end. (1 Corinthians 13:3–7 MSG)

Second Section
The Prophetic, Fivefold Ministry, Seven Mountains of Influence

Why should you learn about prophecy if you are going to make proclamations over the land and not people? Because you have to know the why and how to recognize the direction of the word the Holy Spirit gives you for that land God will call you to minister over.

The prophetic or the gift of prophecy is the ability to proclaim a message from God. The Hebrew term for prophet, *navi*, literally means "spokesperson."[19] A prophet speaks to the people as a mouthpiece of God and to God on behalf of the people. We are not prophets, nor do we claim to be one, but we all hold prophetic gifts. We are filled with the Holy Spirit to bring encouragement and edification and to help bring direction and confirmation to many around us. Prophecy may include offering warnings to an extent that is not hostile to those who need help in any area of their walk with the Lord.

We should speak in ways that can be easily understood after each experience or trial we go through. Pursuing God's love will keep you balanced, and you will hear from God and learn to filter what to say or not to say. It takes experience, so you need to practice hearing and listening (Shema). This is not just for the spiritually mature but is available to everyone. The purpose of prophecy is to encourage and comfort each other as stated in 1 Corinthians 14:3–4: "But the one who prophesies speaks to people for their strengthening, encouraging and comfort. Anyone who speaks in a tongue edifies themselves, but the one who prophesies edifies the church." However, because we are not perfect and we are not without sin, we will always have a partial word. Each word given to a person could be just a portion of a bigger word, and later others may continue that word or confirm it through the course of their lives as illustrated in 1 Corinthians 13:9. " For we know in part, and we prophesy in part" (KJV).

When you are about to give a word, you need to move cautiously. Pray for the person before going forward. You should always have someone record what you say and be expectant in seeing that word come to pass for the person.

I have gained a few insights over the years. Whether with youth or adults, many times, when asking the Lord to show me a prophetic word, the Holy Spirit might reveal to me areas of sin in a person's life, or the hurt, pain, or fear that they may be carrying. (This applies with prophetic words over the land as well.) I would then wait and filter my word. While working the altars at churches and praying for people, I saw their area of struggle first and felt it wasn't my place to tell them of their sin or pain. I would just pray for them.

When I was younger, I blurted out their fears and explained that God does not give them a spirit of fear. But at times, I scared them with my revelation. Over time, I learned what to do and not to do; I should have just connected with their spirit and spoke life to their fear. It was not my place to tell them what they already knew but to project to them the direction they needed to go.

For example, a lady was at the altar waiting for prayer, and as I walked over to her, I saw a picture of her getting into an accident because of her drunk driving. When I reached her, I waited before I opened my mouth. I was then led to tell her not what I had seen, but the *complete opposite*. I began to encourage her regarding this picture. I didn't second guess what the Lord showed me. I said, "I see the Lord holding you, and He believes in you, and He will protect you on the road, driving." I also thanked the Lord for the courage she would need for the next chapters in her life. I told her that we should ask the Lord to give her wisdom and that she would be drawn to the Holy Spirit like never before. If you see negative things, prophesy the opposite. The more you stick to encouragement, the more the Lord will open your mind to receive accurate downloads from him.

When prophesying over the land, the Lord will show you how that region, neighborhood, community, or town is suffering. Different areas may have different struggles, such as suicide, drugs, sex trafficking, robbery, deceit, lies, injustice, abortion, selfish pride, or a religious spirit. Remember, you don't necessarily have to war over these areas in prayer; you just have to position your heart and prophesy over it or lift up a spontaneous song as God leads you.

I strongly advise not to engage in any warfare prayer because you may feel and see all the yucky stuff. Take the humble approach and cry over its pain. Cry to change that atmosphere. Stay within the limits of blessing the land, get in, and get out. Just do what you are called to do. Understanding your authority in Jesus is key because Christ didn't have to fight with anyone. He may have gotten upset, but he knew his place and power. A good understanding is power and confidence. If you are on that ground, you are responsible to utilize your authority over that ground. The Bible tells us that we were connected to the ground on the sixth day of creation. Stay in the realm of what you know; if you are uncertain don't go there. Stick to blessing the land, the people.

David Ministered Over the King

> Now, the Lord's Spirit had left Saul, and an *evil spirit from the Lord* tormented him. Saul's officials told him, "An evil spirit from God is tormenting you. Your Majesty, why don't you command us to look for a man who can play the lyre well? When the evil spirit from God comes to you, he'll strum a tune, and

you'll feel better. "Saul told his officials, "Please find me a man who can play well and bring him to me." One of the officials said, "I know one of Jesse's sons from Bethlehem who can play well. He's a courageous man and a warrior. *He has a way with words,* he is handsome, and the Lord is with him."

Saul sent messengers to Jesse to say, "Send me your son David, who is with the sheep." Jesse took six bushels of bread, a full wineskin, and a young goat and sent them with his son David to Saul. David came to Saul and *served him.* Saul loved him very much and made David his armorbearer. Saul sent this message to Jesse, "Please let David stay with me because I have grown fond of him." Whenever God's spirit came to Saul, David took the lyre and strummed a tune. Saul got relief from his terror and felt better, and the evil spirit left him. (1 Samuel 16:19–23 GOD'S WORD)

Why sing over the *land*? It is ours; we are the forerunners. God has given us the land on which we reside. We come from the Earth; God breathed life into man, and from the dust, man was created. We need to utilize the tools of the Earth, play instruments, and sing over it to change the atmosphere of our region. The Earth will come into agreement with us. Second Chronicles 7:14 gives us a powerful promise that God will change the land: "If my people, who are called by my name, will humble themselves and pray and seek my face and turn from their wicked ways, then I will hear from heaven, and I will forgive their sin and will heal their land."

Third-Heaven Living

Is third-heaven living biblical? There are three heavens, according to the Bible. The first heaven is where the birds and airplanes fly. The second heaven is the celestial heaven where the sun, moon, and stars are. The third heaven is God's dwelling place. In the prophet Jeremiah's vision, he speaks of "the heavens," not heaven (Jeremiah 4:23). Additionally, the Bible mentions "the first heaven" and "the third heaven," so we must believe there is second heaven. Other Scriptures that speak of the heavens include Deuteronomy 10:14; 1 Kings 8:27. In some places, the Bible just says "heaven." "I know a man in Christ who fourteen years ago was caught up to the third heaven. Whether it was in the body or out of the body I do not know—God knows. And I know that this man—whether in the body or apart from the body I do not know, but God knows—was caught up to paradise and heard inexpressible things, things that no one is permitted to tell" (2 Corinthians 12:2–4).

Third heaven is an understanding. *It's an understanding*, a positional stance, so when we pray your prayer is coming from a place of heaven, thanking him for that which has already been done in heaven as it will be done on Earth. We ascend with our spiritual being into high places, positioning our hearts in all trials and situations of victory. We are full of love and confidence that what is done in heaven will be done on Earth; the third heaven ministering to the first heaven, Earth. This all happens in our minds and is manifested in our hearts and souls. We hope in the things we don't see but have the full faith of their deliverance. (See Hebrews 11:1.) Could it be that simple? Yes. We stay clear of the distractions we may see in the second heaven; we don't fight the spiritual forces or demons or what we don't understand. We don't put targets on our backs and knock on doors we should not be knocking on. There is a right time and place for that.

The Fivefold Ministry

"So Christ himself gave the apostles, the prophets, the evangelists, the pastors and teachers, to equip his people for works of service, so that the body of Christ may be built up" (Ephesians 4:11–12).

The fivefold ministry of the church, that is, the role of apostles, prophets, evangelists, pastors, and teachers is described in Ephesians 4. We must have an idea of who we are to understand where we are going. We all carry each of these roles or gifts, but some are stronger than others:
- **Apostle:** the dream awakener—calls forth our calling in God
- **Prophet:** the heart revealer—reveals the heart of God and men
- **Evangelist:** the storyteller—helps us understand the story of God in the context of current relevance

- **Pastor:** the soul healer—comes alongside to repair our souls
- **Teacher:** the light giver—helps us to look at life, opens up the Scripture to show that Jesus has a plan and instruction for practical living[20]

Why focus on these five ministries? Revelation 19:7 says the Bride of his saints are "ready." These five ministries build up the saints, prepare the way, and equip yourselves and others. You can go online to take a test to evaluate your ministry strengths. This will allow others who work with you or serve you to better understand your role. The test may not turn out how you expect it to, but it will give you a great idea of your strengths if you don't know them by now. However, over time you will be able to operate in all five areas of ministry. Here's a website to take the test and find out your results: https://www.fivefoldministry.com/survey-answer-set/120109/results.

When you receive your test results, see if they resonate with you. If not, don't worry as you may not yet be working in that area of ministry. You might work in that area at a later time in life. Even so, you will definitely see your strong points.

The Seven Mountains of Societal Influence

These seven spheres (mountains) of influence are religion, family, education, government, media, arts and entertainment, and business. We first heard about the "Seven Spheres of Influence" from an evangelical who brought so much understanding to this topic back in the 1970s.[21] Instead of separating ourselves from the world, we need to be a part of these mountains as the influencers. Not to change the mountains, but to be a part of them and influence them. Some in the church believe we should dominate the culture, but I felt led in my walk to be a model in these areas, working from the inside out. Here are the seven areas of influence.

1. **Religion:** The church, no matter what denomination—your church or another church—serves as a model.
2. **Family**: These organizations help and influence families to better their lives. They don't have to be Christian establishments, such as Boys and Girls Clubs or family counseling in public schools. Your influence can change the atmosphere.

3. **Education:** Public schools need more Christian role models to make a difference in the lives of the students they teach.
4. **Government:** Be a Christian in politics and model Jesus; you don't have to be excessively vocal about him but should model his life and influence the culture.
5. **Media:** Media includes journalism, television, webhosting, podcasts, and more. Some Christians prefer to focus on faith-based media, but secular companies are lacking God's love as well.
6. **Arts and Entertainment:** Movies can model strong Christian values and integrity without including Scripture in their dialogue. Again, model positive movies by showing how Christ lived.
7. **Business:** Open a business and share Christian ways that will connect—not separate—godly individuals with those who have not yet come to Christ. Invite them to be a part. Not all places are as outspoken as Chick-fil-A, the popular fast-food restaurant known for their Christian beliefs and upstanding values.[22]

We should strive to be excellent in all areas of our influence. Daniel 6:3 says, "Then this Daniel became distinguished above all the other high officials and satraps, because an *excellent spirit was in him*. And the king planned to set him over the whole kingdom." The root of the word "excellent" comes from the Hebrew word *yateer*, which means "to rise to the top."[23] God instilled an excellent spirit in Daniel. This allowed him to rise to the top of the mountain God called him to influence—the government.

With the Holy Spirit inside us, we have the power and the energy to impact the world around us. Just as Daniel stepped into his sphere of the kingdom, so we can step into the world around us. How can you make a big social impact? Determine the mountain of influence you are called to:

- What mountain am I called to serve?
- What gifts has God given me to use there?
- What resources and connections do I have?
- What fuels and inspires me in this mountain?
- What strengths have others affirmed in me?

These questions, along with listening to the Holy Spirit, will help direct you to the mountain God has given you.

1. **Determine how to impact your mountain.** Daniel's excellent spirit and his ability to rise to the top is exactly what you are called to do. How will you do this well? You will need to set goals and develop a specific game plan in order to impact the mountain God calls you to.
2. **Faithfully impact your mountain.** When you have identified your mountain and have a plan for influencing it, you can then effectively step into the work of impacting your mountain. This includes continually learning about how to best make an impact as well as following your plan and listening to the Holy Spirit as he directs your steps. Start, but move forward slowly in this process. Answer these questions.
- How will you be faithful to serve your mountain?
- What will you do (modeling Christ) to bring the mentality of the kingdom to Earth?
- What goals do you need to establish to impact your mountain?

Third Section
Small Group Meetings

Lessen 1

Starting your small groups: When starting your small group or family meeting you need to respect the honesty and the openness of everyone who is attending. Maintain confidentiality and keep conversations within the walls of the meeting. It creates a safe atmosphere to share with ease.

Suggested Meeting Agenda
- **Welcome and prayer:** Welcome everyone and have someone else say the opening prayer. This lets others know you are inviting a conversation in your session and builds trust.
- **Introduce group members:** Give members chance to talk about themselves and their families. Where are members from? Give them the time to share.

- **Ask how long group members have been Christians:** This is vital so you can adjust your teaching and slow down if you need to help those who are new to biblical understanding. Veterans in the Word can sit next to new believers to help them along.
- **Learn what members hope to get out of the sessions:** You can then help address what you will cover and try to bring a clear understanding to what you need to teach. Have members write their goals on paper and give them to you. Review these during the next meeting.
- **Model honesty and transparency:** Be honest and let members know you don't have all the answers. You can learn together. Please don't come across like a know-it-all, because we should carry the heart of a learner.
- **Encourage taking notes and jotting down Scriptures:** The Holy Spirit will drop in, and a person may have a word for someone else, so be prepared to write it down or videotape it on your phone.

Lesson 2

- **Share your testimony:** As the leader of the group, be prepared to share your own testimony. In our case, we were called to bring awareness on suicide and faith because we were dealing with this area in our family. We were called to sing over and prophesy over the land where God assigned us, including Ireland, Hawaii, and Seattle where we felt called to minister. I shared about our struggles with our sons, our testimony, and what we learned from it. We learned to listen to God, Shema. But share about whatever area you are dealing with as you feel led by the Holy Spirit or even areas that you are working through to move into claiming victory over your family. That is only done by faith.

Lesson 3

Scripture to study: 1 Corinthians 13:4–7

SHEMA

This session is filled with questions to review with everyone and group interaction. For a smaller group, you can spend time here. If you have a larger group, watch your time. This is a place of love. Remember to utilize this Scripture to answer from your perspective rather than looking at another person who has shown you these attributes. Reflect on how well we try to love like Christ does. Knowing the answers to these questions will help you when you are faced with choosing to speak life over people when you have the opportunity.

If I give everything I own to the poor and even go to the stake to be burned as a martyr, but I don't love, I've gotten nowhere. So, no matter what I say, what I believe, and what I do, I'm bankrupt without love.

1. Love never gives up:
2. Love cares more for others than for self:
3. Love doesn't want what it doesn't have,
4. Love doesn't strut,
5. Doesn't have a swelled head,
6. Doesn't force itself on others,
7. Isn't always "me first,"
8. Doesn't fly off the handle,
9. Doesn't keep score of the sins of others,
10. Doesn't revel when others grovel,
11. Takes pleasure in the flowering of truth,
12. Puts up with anything,
13. Trusts God always,
14. Always looks for the best,
15. Never looks back,
16. But keeps going to the end. (1 Corinthians 13:4–7 MSG)

As you can see, the above Bible passage listed sixteen examples of love. Again, during this session, reflect on each topic and answer it by providing your own personal experience. Secondly, think about that person who has expressed that topic in their life. Talk about it and be mindful of how God's love, big or small, can impact your heart by just talking. I have given you an example from my life, but you have seventeen examples of love to choose from. You can choose several or just do them all.

Sample Reflection Question: From your life experience

Have you ever demonstrated the ability to never give up on somebody?

Love never gives up: When I first married Joseph, I was pregnant at a young age. I received my diploma while three months pregnant. It was a rough time for me as I felt shame and was afraid of my future. Despite all the happy faces, I was sad that I let my parents down and had to forfeit my scholarship. As young parents, we often wanted to give up; we both wanted to throw in the towel. We realized it wasn't an option because we had our firstborn to care for. It wasn't just us anymore; it was all about him. Joseph put his career on hold, and so did I, but we never gave up on our son.

Sample Reflection Question:
Who has shown or modeled love that never gives up to you?

Lesson 4

The Discipline of Listening

Let's practice and reflect on how well you listen. This is a writing lesson, so get your pen and paper ready to jot down what you hear. Ask the question and take time to hear him and write down your answer. Ask the Holy Spirit to help you to hear spiritually. He talks with pictures, colors, single words, Scriptures, animal characteristics, songs, movies, television, and more. He can speak in endless ways.

- When you woke up, what was God saying to you before you started your day?
- What is he saying to you about your surroundings?
- What is he saying about where you live, even in your county?
- About the people?
- About the school system?
- About the finances in your state?
- Teenagers? Your congregation?
- Your job?
- The Earth?

Practice listening to what God could be saying in your surroundings. Ponder on these questions; God is speaking all the time. Usually He's preparing for you to share what he's saying with someone later in your day.

Lesson 5

The Practice of Hearing God

Hearing God's voice doesn't come easy for some; you must practice this. Jesus modeled the prophetic with the disciples. The church and the prophetic overall isn't just hearing from God but walking it out. Jesus didn't know Zacchaeus. He received a word of knowledge about Zacchaeus's life, and he didn't keep that knowledge to himself. Jesus walked it out by sharing it publicly. Luke 19:5 describes their encounter: "When Jesus reached the spot, he looked up and said to him, 'Zacchaeus, come down immediately. I must stay at your house today.'"

Here, Jesus demonstrated knowing about Zacchaeus before they even met. This shows the power and the mysteries that are available for us through the prophetic.

God will show up in everything if we are open to how he speaks to us. He speaks in the air, in the sea, through nature, objects, colors, moments in time, situations, through other people, movies, colors, numbers, buildings, animals, dreams, people's actions, scenarios from life events, through Scripture, through babies, and more.

A word of prophecy tells the future or reveals purpose. Jesus came to restore all things. You may be someone's fire starter, so when you hear from God, you can help them on their way to their future. The message of 1 Corinthians 14:11 is to speak in ways that can be understood. We are to pursue love and desire spiritual gifts, but especially the gift of speaking what God has revealed. Do not doubt that God is talking to you. Trust that he is because he waits for you to meet up with him in everything every day. Deuteronomy 31:8 says he will go before you: "The Lord himself goes before you and will be with you; he will never leave you nor forsake you. Do not be afraid; do not be discouraged."

Assemble the Barn Owls: A Call to Shift the Atmosphere of Regions

Listening Exercise

Your exercise here is to listen to the sky and what is it saying. Listen to the land in your region. What is it saying? Listen to the water, the ocean, the river. What are they saying to you? I know this seems unusual but practice hearing what the elements are saying around you. They carry so many mysteries and secrets that you can use in understanding how you need to pray. Anything that keeps you away from practicing the prophetic is not from God. Salvation and receiving Jesus into your life was a prophetic act. We were made to share spiritual information from the Lord. The sheep hear his voice. When you share your belief in Him, you are engaging in a prophetic act.

Lesson 6

Listen to the Holy Spirit

This lesson will give you a chance to interact with a partner, to pray, to wait and listen and to give a word to your partner.

Give each person around the table a chance to listen to the Holy Spirit. You can even choose partners. Simply ask the Holy Spirit to show you what he wants to show you to bless this person. He may reveal a color, a picture, an object, a number, anything. Try not to think too hard because usually the first picture that comes to mind is what he wants you to share.

Then look at your partner and say what you see and hear. Don't try to understand it. The message is not for you; it's for them. You will be the mediator. Remind them it's okay to make mistakes and let them know it's okay for to bring correction. You need to lead to help them understand. You can also help bring confirmation by providing Scriptures attached to a prophetic word.

When I am teaching a class, I begin with worship. I invite the Holy Spirit to help us receive what He wants us to receive. We would spend time in his presence. I would then start to call up one person at a time to practice and give a word. We would agree that we were learning together and be open to correction by sharing with all. I would do this with the youth. I never intended to humiliate them or bring shame during the learning process as we learned together.

Joseph played the guitar while I was on the mic. I would call up a person, have them pray a short prayer, and ask them who the Lord was leading them to give a word to. I would guide them through prophesying to that person. They would be scared, but I would ask them, "What is the Holy Spirit saying?" Before they answered, I advised them to wait if they received a word of warning and say the opposite to bring comfort, healing, and encouragement. This was such a fun time. We would go on for hours.

After every teaching, we would pray and worship or have a snack and continue the next week with Holy Spirit games, like partnering up and asking the Holy Spirit for specific insights on people as we prayed for them and practiced listening.

I would play a game with my kids to see if they were listening to the Holy Spirit. We would sit at the table and draw a picture or write a word from the Holy Spirit. Later we would discuss what they thought that picture meant and how we could use it today to help encourage others or ourselves.

We are made to be interactive with Gods presence. What I just shared with you in this chapter is a simple way to practice the prophetic. This is just a start, and the more you learn about it, the more you will find yourself becoming a seasoned encourager to be used for god's purpose in your everyday life. If you wish to learn more about the prophetic, search it out, I do. There is so much more you can learn about it; we just covered the surface.

FINAL THOUGHTS

Through our walk with the Lord, we have discovered that we love his presence so much that it is a cherished lifestyle. I love each one of my kids and hope they will pursue the Lord and continue to tap into his presence, the Ruach Hakodesh.

I also encourage you to find his voice in everything you do and watch how God will open your relationship and bring it to new levels of hearing and understanding. I thank God for my mom and dad who gave us the opportunity at a young age to really experience the throne room of God through worship. We will continue the legacy and continue our covenant agreements concerning worship over the land.

I also honor all the churches where we served. We learned a lot as we fell into God's embrace. We grew closer to God in ways we never dreamed possible. We served next to remarkable men and women of the faith that we dearly love to this day. One particular friend has been my witness through all that we have been through. Brianna, thank you for all the prayers and the encouragement that you gave to hold me up in times when I felt defeated. You have witnessed all the hardship and pain we went through. I love you, sis!

Last, but not least, to the man of my life, Joseph. I thank God for you. It has been an incredible ride, baby, and we were truly destined to be with each other. I love how we both enjoy encouraging and teaching others to walk out their life with God's presence.

Special Love to Ellen and Lisa for making this dream come to life.

Let your Shema begin, and let us start to blow the trumpet and assemble the spiritual barn owls. Joseph and I commission you to walk out your destiny. Find a good church and begin to worship and prophesy over your region. Let us Shema together.

ENDNOTES

1　Hebrew 4 Christians, "The Shema – Hear, O Israel," accessed January 19, 2021, https://hebrew4christians.com/Scripture/Torah/The_Shema/the_shema.html.

2　Jeff A. Benner, Ancient Hebrew Research Center, "What is Torah?" accessed January 19, 2021, https://www.ancient-hebrew.org/studies-words/what-is-torah.htm.

3　Living Word in 3-D, "Ruach HaKodesh: The Holy Spirit," accessed January 19, 2021, http://livingwordin3d.com/discovery/2018/08/09/ruach-hakodesh-the-holy-spirit.

4　Ibid.

5　Ibid.

6　Ibid.

7　History, "Two airplanes collide over New York City," accessed January 19, 2021, https://www.history.com/this-day-in-history/two-airplanes-collide-over-new-york-city.

8　Hebrew 4 Christians, "Hebrew Names of God," accessed January 19, 2021, https://www.hebrew4christians.com/Names_of_G-d/Spirit_of_God/spirit_of_god.html.

9　Ali Gordon, "Biggest brood of barn owls recorded near Lough Neagh," BBC News, July 27, 2018, https://www.bbc.com/news/uk-northern-ireland-44971883.

10　Sorcha Pollack, "Storm Ali brought strongest gust recorded by Galway station – weather report," The Irish Times, October 2, 2018, https://www.irishtimes.com/news/environment/storm-ali-brought-strongest-gust-recorded-by-galway-station-weather-report-1.3649216.

11　Brojure, "The Rock of Cashel," accessed January 19, 2021, https://brojure.com/reiimagine-social-media/ireland-destination-guide/a/205941/the-rock-of-cashel.

12	Ibid. http://www.megalithicireland.com/St%20Lassair's%20Holy%20Well,%20Kilronan.html.
13	Ibid.
14	Denis Carroll, "Fr Michael O'Flanagan, 1876-1942: A Priest for the People." The Furrow 43, no. 10 (1992): 547–50. Accessed January 19, 2021. http://www.jstor.org/stable/27662276.
15	Carrow keel, "From Cliffony to Crosna: Fr. Michael O'Flanagan," accessed January 19, 2021, http://www.carrowkeel.com/frof/main.html.
16	Ibid. http://www.carrowkeel.com/frof/inventions.html.
17	Hebrew 4 Christians, "The Letter Dalet," accessed January 19, 2021, https://www.hebrew4christians.com/Grammar/Unit_One/Aleph-Bet/Dalet/dalet.html.
18	All About God, "Gifts of the Spirit," accessed January 19, 2021, https://www.allaboutgod.com/gifts-of-the-spirit.htm.
19	Yona Sabar, Jewish Journal, "Hebrew Word of the Week: navi' 'prophet,'" April 14, 2017, https://jewishjournal.com/culture/217909/hebrew-word-week-navi-prophet.
20	Fivefold Ministry, "Fivefold Ministry Test," accessed January 19, 2021, https://fivefoldministry.com/static/learn-about-the-five-fold-ministry.
21	Youth With a Mission, "Transforming Spheres of Society," November 8, 2016, https://ywam.org/uncategorized/transforming-spheres-of-society.
22	Ibid.
23	Blue Letter Bible, "Lexicon :: Strong's H3335 – yatsar," accessed January 19, 2021, https://www.blueletterbible.org/lang/lexicon/lexicon.cfm?t=kjv&strongs=h3335.

Made in the USA
Monee, IL
07 March 2021